FRANKIE & BOBBY:
The Rest of Our Story

FRANKIE & BOBBY:
The Rest of Our Story

BOB ZAPPA
WITH DIANE E. PAPALIA

© 2017 Charles R. Zappa
All rights reserved.

ISBN: 1544258798
ISBN 13: 9781544258799

This book is dedicated:

To Carl Zappa and Candy Zappa-Porter, for sharing their lives with me, and our brother, Frank.

To Stanley Jason Zappa, for showing me the true meaning of strength of character in the face of adversity.

To Moon Zappa, Dweezil Zappa, and Megan Zappa, for giving me the opportunity to be a part of their lives.

And especially to my best friend, coauthor, wife, and love of my life, Diane Papalia Zappa, for making this the best time of our lives.

Advance Praise

THE FOLLOWING INDIVIDUALS are intimately familiar with Frank's music and career. Their comments about this book will help set the stage for what you are about to read. My thanks to Professor Joe Klein, composer and conductor Ed Palermo, and linguist and Zappanale master of ceremonies, Jim Cohen, for their insight and thoughtful reviews.

I loved Bob Zappa's first memoir about his life with his older brother, Frank. It was the only book ever written about Frank Zappa's childhood years, written by the only person qualified to do that.

Like many customers of that book, I assume the only regret we had was the story ended in 1967. I wanted to keep reading!

Well, this sequel more than fulfills that desire. *Frankie & Bobby: The Rest of Our Story* picks up where *Frankie & Bobby: Growing Up Zappa* leaves off. In this new one, we follow Bob's life and career choices, all the while being privy to older brother Frank's snarky but caring advice. Bob takes us backstage at monumental Zappa shows with inside stories that only he can tell. This book is every bit as charming and insightful as the first one.

But then it gets dark. We learn about some very disturbing maneuvers surrounding Frank's illness and eventual demise. One can imagine the emotional pain that comes with being kept out of the loop when a loved one is suffering with a terminal illness. This book answers many questions all of us Zappaphiles have asked since that fateful day we lost Frank.

Frankie & Bobby: The Rest of Our Story ends on a very optimistic beat, mainly due to Bob's reunion with nephew Dweezil and niece Moon. We also learn a lot about their past and current tribulations with the Zappa estate.

"*Frankie & Bobby: The Rest of Our Story*" is a must-read!

—Ed Palermo, Composer and Leader of Ed Palermo's Big Band

Who'd have thought when Frank and Bobby Zappa parted ways at the end of Bob Zappa's first book, *Frankie & Bobby: Growing Up Zappa*, that there would be so much more of their story to tell? With this equally engaging sequel, *Frankie & Bobby: The Rest of Our Story*, Bob Zappa fills even more gaps in his brother's biography, with touching vignettes of how their lives intermittently intersected over the last decades of Frank's life.

As with Bob's first book, *The Rest of Our Story* paints an evocative portrait of life in America through the author's personal anecdotes, this time beginning with the Vietnam era through the present day. Along the way, Frank makes a number of appearances, as critical points in the iconic musician's life and career are set in relief from the perspective of his brother Bob's own path—the latter of which resonates more with us "regular folks," for whom Frank's extraordinary life in the public eye would seem to be such a foreign experience.

Perhaps most poignant are the episodes relating to Frank's own family—in particular his wife, Gail, and her increasingly irrational behavior during the final years of Frank's life. If for no other reason, Bob's unflinching account of that strange relationship is significant in shedding a stark light on a matter that has baffled and frustrated the Zappa fan community for decades. Bob's and his family's banishment from the lives of Frank and his kids is a bizarre and heartbreaking tale. The silver lining to it all is the moving reunion of Moon and Dweezil with their uncle and his family following Gail's death, after more than four decades of imposed estrangement. *Frankie & Bobby: The Rest of Our Story* is another must-read for any Zappologist curious for answers regarding some of the more enigmatic aspects of Frank's life.

—**Joseph Klein, DMus**
Distinguished Teaching Professor
Chair, Division of Composition Studies
University of North Texas
Denton, Texas

A memoir is more than recollection; it exposes a continuum of related events. Bob Zappa's *Frankie & Bobby: The Rest of Our Story* is wisdom gained over time. Picking up where his first book left off, it focuses on Bob's adventures in the United States and elsewhere, including a Swedish university course in deviant behavior and a close brush with Soviet espionage. Bob's ultimate purpose of understanding how his alienation from his brother Frank's world developed, or was created, overshadows these episodes.

Climaxing with a series of rejections relating to the passing of their mother, Rose Marie, and finally of Frank himself, Bob celebrates his subsequent reconciliation with Dweezil and Moon and a new life rooted deep in his past. Bob's second book ends with an open message to his brother that was undoubtedly the beginning of the entire project. The response will have to wait for another world—with room service, we hope. A great read, and for the Zappa faithful, optimistic closure.

—James Cohen, Zappanale Master
of Ceremonies since 1999

Contents

Advance Praise · vii
Foreword · xiii
Acknowledgments · xv
Introduction · xvii

1	Frank Returns to Los Angeles ·	1
2	Stockholm and the Potty Poster ·	11
3	My Russian Holiday Adventure ·	19
4	How I Almost Became a Russian Spy ·	31
5	Back to Los Angeles ·	41
6	When Working in Publishing Was Cool ·	47
7	New York, the Second Time Around ·	57
8	Publish or Perish ·	63
9	Frank and Smothers Visit McGraw-Hill ·	69
10	Mamma Zappa Goes to Mamma Leone's · · · · · · · · · · · · · · · · ·	75
11	Frank, Smothers, and Bobby in New Orleans · · · · · · · · · · · · · · ·	81
12	Frank Plays the Saenger Auditorium in New Orleans · · · · · · · ·	87
13	Why Can't I See My Brother? ·	93
14	Frank's Death and Its Aftermath ·	101
15	Was Frank Zappa a Genius? ·	113

16	Frank Zappa: Tributes and Honors	123
17	Reconnecting with Moon and Dweezil	131
18	Bob Zappa Today	143

A Few Last Words ·········· 157
About the Authors ·········· 159

Foreword

by Co de Kloet

Bob Zappa's first book, *Frankie & Bobby: Growing Up Zappa*, was a great read and a beautiful "painting" of an era I never experienced. His second book is just as enjoyable.

Frank was, as everybody with good taste and insight knows, a phenomenon impossible to describe. Many writers and filmmakers tried to grasp his uniqueness, and while many did nice jobs, not all got it right. Many forgot to mention that Frank often referred to himself as "a regular guy."

And that is the force of this book. By sharing personal, sometimes extremely intimate stories about his relationship with Frank, Bob gives us a clear view of that regular-guyness quality, leaving the importance and impact of his brother's life intact. By not just focusing on Frank and giving us information about other relations and some of his own experiences, Bob puts Frank in a new and sincere perspective. I had a great time reading it, and I hope it will do well.

Over the years, I had a friendship with Herbie Cohen, Frank's manager and business partner. He was at my farmhouse a few times, and once when he was reading something in a book about Zappa, he smiled and said, "It is always fun to read what people *think* really happened [in Frank's life], but they haven't got a clue." Bob Zappa has! And that is what makes this book a must-have. Thanks, Bob, and thanks as always, Frank.

About Co de Kloet

Co de Kloet is a well-known radio personality and music producer in Amsterdam. He had a long, personal relationship with Frank starting in 1977 until Frank's death in 1993. "My relationship with one of the great music icons of our time, Frank Zappa, cannot be fully told because there are simply too many personal stories," de Kloet says. "I miss him daily, and he was, is, and always will be a very important factor in my personal and professional life. I am proud to say that my relationship with Frank lives on through his highly talented son Dweezil."

Acknowledgments

This book is a memoir. It contains thoughts and images that describe the events that took place during a specific period in the lives of my brother Frank and me. Some names have been changed to protect the identities of the individuals who played a role in those events. Dialogue that appears in the text is my best recollection of what was said. It is a work intended to help readers understand the relationship that Frank and I had from 1967 to the time of his death.

Introduction

For those of you who read my first book, *Frankie & Bobby: Growing Up Zappa*, thank you. I hope you enjoyed it and found that the information about Frank added to your understanding of his complex and brilliant mind and his early development. This book tells the next chapter in our story.

"At a book signing at the Gold Million Records music and bookstore in Bryn Mawr, Pennsylvania, with Brandon Montemorano of Queens, New York."

It's about how my brother and I continued on our separate but intertwined paths after his successful long-running show, *Absolutely Freee* (sic), at the Garrick Theater in New York in the summer of 1967.

That was a monumental time for me. I learned a lot about myself, but more importantly, I witnessed firsthand Frank's emergence as a professional musician, entertainer, and social critic. What I learned about myself back then was that I didn't belong in the music business. Not just in rock and roll, but in any other facet of that artistic medium. My interests leaned more toward activities with much lower volume and quieter surroundings. Besides, I had abandoned any hope of learning how to play guitar, and even though I liked the sound of another instrument, the accordion, it had no place in rock and roll either. Just kidding!

I also learned that life on the road was a mixed blessing for Frank. He once told me that his ideal vacation was room service in a nice hotel. Food was an added bonus. Having time away from his family was part of the mixed blessing too. He missed his kids and the solitude of his studio and basement workshop. He missed the comforts of the home he bought in 1968 and that he lived in until his death in 1993.

Given our childhood history of many family moves, twenty-five years in the same place was a singular achievement for him. But he was a musician, and musicians go where the audiences are. And Frank's listeners were all over the world.

My goal in telling you this part of our story is to describe some of the other personal and private components to Frank's complex personality as I remember them. For example, when he was at the

Parents Music Resource Center Hearing in Washington in 1985, he made the comment that the media "write about me like I'm a maniac…I'm not. I'm forty years old. I've got four kids and a mortgage."

In that moment, Frank was like so many other men with prosperous careers. He did what he did because he was very good at it and because he liked doing it. Some journalists, radio, and TV news reporters found him fair game for their snarky articles or patronizing sound bites. Serious investigative journalists wrote about him based on what he had accomplished, not because of his appearance.

Talking heads on television tried to pigeonhole him into dinnertime TV news segments, while radio talk show people thought they could get away with blindsiding him for paltry ratings bumps, only to find themselves outclassed, outthought, and backpedaling when they came across like buffoons. Frank was a champion of free thought, artistic integrity, and no-bullshit politics.

The presidential election of 2016 would have given him so much grist that I think the media would have devoted much coverage to his unique and eloquent insights. A good example of these is in the documentary *Eat That Question*, from German director Thorsten Schutte. It captures Frank's responses to interviewer questions at different stages of his career, even toward the end of his life.

In a review I wrote for the film, I explained that on Monday night (June 20, 2016), when my wife, Diane, and I met up with her daughter, Anna, at the Landmark Theater in New York, we went to the ticket booth to ask for Gary Springer, the man in charge of PR for the movie.

The young woman in the booth didn't know Gary, so I said, "We're here to see the preview of the Sony movie."

And she said, "You mean the one about Frank Kafka?"

And therein lies the mystery that is Frank Zappa. It's not that people can't pronounce our last name. It's that too many people still don't know how brilliant, talented, and outspoken Frank was. This biopic will help correct that.

"Moon with me at a special showing of Eat That Question in New York City on Monday, June 20, 2016."

The documentary is a montage of interviews, performances, and video clips that give viewers an intimate look into Frank's passion for artistic integrity and free speech and his utter disdain of religious intolerance, political and social oppression, and any bias against free thought. It depicts how Frank had the verbal agility and intellectual depth to back up his convictions. He was self-taught in many areas, so well read and technically sophisticated.

My niece Moon Zappa wanted to know if parts of the film would sadden me. (When you see it, you'll know which ones I mean.)

And I told her that I wouldn't miss it, sadness notwithstanding. But I planned to bring a box of Kleenex with me just in case.

Growing up with Frank and sharing so many adventures with him will always be a cherished memory for me. Describing our lives in this memoir, as well as in my first book, has been a rewarding experience. Reliving our family history, adolescence, and adult situations has helped me come to terms with my relationship with one of the most creative, influential, and prolific artists of the twentieth century.

Over the years, Frank and I were very close. He was my best friend and my source of clear thinking and brotherly guidance. He was also the inspiration for the hopes, expectations, and courage of so many others who were—or are even now—the hungry freaks he so ably championed. I hope this book will add to the body of information about Frank Zappa so that future generations won't confuse him with a nineteenth-century Czech novelist or with anyone else, because he was a true original, the likes of which will not been seen again.

—Charles R. "Bob" Zappa

1

Frank Returns to Los Angeles

> *We...moved into a large log cabin once owned by old-time cowboy star Tom Mix at the corner of Laurel Canyon Boulevard and Lookout Mountain Drive. The living room was seventy-five by thirty feet with a large fireplace.*
>
> —Frank Zappa, *The Real Frank Zappa Book*

Nineteen sixty-seven was an interesting year. By year's end, the Dow Jones Industrial Average was 905. The average cost of a new house was $14,250. The average income was $7,300. Gas was $0.33 per gallon back then. The average cost of a new car was $2,750. The federal minimum wage was $1.40.

Thurgood Marshall was appointed the first African American Supreme Court justice, the Beatles released *Sgt. Pepper's Lonely Hearts Club Band*, the very first issue of *Rolling Stone* magazine was published, and US Navy pilot and now senator John McCain was shot down over North Vietnam and spent five and a half years in a Vietnamese prison.

It was the best of times for some, but for others, it was really awful. For me, though, life was good. I was back in California, back in college, working part time, and going to the beach when time allowed.

We Resume Our Story When...

In late August 1967, after working for Frank at the Garrick Theater in Greenwich Village for almost two months, I made the decision to go back to California to finish college. But while I was with him that summer, the shows he and the Mothers of Invention did were amazing performances that helped establish Frank as a phenomenon in the rock music business.

Looking back, I remember how my adventure in rock and roll began. Near the end of April 1967, Frank called me from New York and asked if I'd be interested in coming to work for him for the summer. He was about a month into the *Absolutely Freee* (sic) show at the Garrick Theater.

I asked, "What do you want me to do?"

He said, "What I need is for you to buy me cigarettes and coffee, and I want to see if you can cut it in the music business. If so, you have to decide if you want to work for me full time."

I asked, "Could you use additional help?"

He asked, "Who do you have in mind?"

I said, "My friends Bill Harris and Dick Barber. You knew them from our days in Claremont."

He paused a minute and then said, "Bring them along, and I'll see if I can find a place for them."

So that June, Bill, Dick, and I set out for New York. It took us about five days to drive cross-country.

Dick Barber is a master mechanic. He knows about engines, transmissions, and electronics, and he has even built and flies his own airplane. He was the kind of rock-steady, technically proficient person that Frank really needed in his entourage. In fact, Dick remained with Frank long after Bill and I left him. As the experience wore on, it became clear that I wasn't cut out for a life on the road, even if it was with Frank.

After leaving him, I was disappointed in myself for not having the temperament for, or enough interest in, the music business to stick with it. But I knew if I stayed, I would become a burden to him and would probably grow unhappier with my role, which wasn't much to begin with, so I chose a different path.

My friend Bill also decided to pack it in. He had already graduated from Claremont McKenna College, and although he was very much interested in the entertainment industry, "gofer" work was not for him.

One day, after Bill and I talked about where we were in the scheme of things with the Mothers, we sat down with Frank.

I began by saying, "As much as Bill and I wish we could have made a go of it with you, we're throwing in the towel."

Frank was very gracious when he heard the news and asked us both to reconsider. But my mind was made up, as was Bill's, so Frank bought us tickets back to Los Angeles, and the next day, we were on an American Airlines flight home.

Thinking back, I have mixed feelings. Not because of the fame Frank achieved or the exciting life he lived, which I could have shared, if only in a small way, but because I was no longer as close to my brother. And given the events in his life in the years following, I felt guilty for having given up so soon.

What Was I Missing?

Not long after I returned to Los Angeles, on September 28, 1967, Moon Unit Zappa, Frank's first child, was born in New York City. I remember him telling me how it changed his life.

He said, "I don't want to make the same mistakes our father made with us."

Moon was the apple of his eye, and he adored her. Time would tell if he fulfilled his promise.

During that time, other things happened that helped establish Frank as a rising star in the music and media business. There was the band's first European tour, the release of *We're Only in It for the Money*, the follow-up release of *Cruising with Ruben and the Jets*, and his foray into the advertising business with his company NTB (Nifty, Tough & Bitchen), which did commercials for Hagstrom guitars and Luden's cough drops. He was on fire.

This was also when he and his business manager, Herbie Cohen, formed Bizarre Records and Straight Records, two labels they used to produce other artists like Captain Beefheart (a.k.a. Don Vliet) and Alice Cooper.

In 1968, after the European tour and launching his other business endeavors, Frank and the Mothers returned to Los Angeles. I really looked forward to seeing him again. He had enough money to rent a place in the Laurel Canyon area, which at the time was a hippie mecca in the Hollywood Hills.

The place he rented was the former home of Tom Mix, an early cowboy-movie hero. The house Tom built around the turn of the century was known in the hippie community as the log cabin because, in fact, it looked like a log cabin. Inside, the house was musty, dark, and poorly furnished.

A one-lane bowling alley was in the basement, and there was rumor of an underground passageway beneath Laurel Canyon Boulevard that led into the basement of Harry Houdini's house across the street. I never found it, though, and I doubt that anyone else did either. The living room was enormous and had a huge fireplace. The basement space was big enough for the band to rehearse in, and there were also two walk-in safes, like bank vaults. A sub-basement, which may have been a wine cellar, had its own spooky quality. Outside, it gave the impression of a foreboding, out-of-place rustic dwelling that could have been used in a horror movie.

And yet Frank was paying $700 a month to live in that badly run-down landmark. After he moved there with his wife, Gail, and daughter, Moon, it quickly became the place to visit if you were in any way connected to the rock music scene. Mick Jagger and Maryann Faithful visited, as did so many other musicians and celebrities. Gawkers and hangers-on tried to gain entry too, some making it and others not. For Frank, the carnival atmosphere began to get old very fast.

In 1968, I was a junior in college and worked part time at the Veterans Administration office in Westwood. The office wasn't far from the log cabin, and I would visit Frank on my way home from work. Once when I stopped by, Frank was holding court with Alice Cooper and other people from the music business. I sat quietly listening to them talk about their shows, other musicians, and record company executives.

At one point, Frank asked Gail, "Can you get me some coffee?"

Everyone in the room watched as she went into the kitchen, most likely expecting her to bring out a pot for all to share. But when she came back with only one cup, I watched as everyone in the room watched Frank drink it between drags on his Winston. In those days, hospitality and social convention in the Frank Zappa household were in short supply.

Before I left that day, Frank pulled me aside and asked me to call his ex-wife, Kay Sherman. He said, "Give her my number and ask her to call me."

I passed on his number to Kay, but I never knew what came of that. Maybe he wanted to see if she knew about his growing fame as a musician. Or maybe he just wanted to talk with a woman who didn't see herself as a ball-squeezing groupie or somebody foolish enough to think she was, simply by association, important in the music business.

After a few months in the log cabin, having grown tired of the constant parade of visitors, hangers-on, and all-around crazies, Frank bought a house on Woodrow Wilson Drive, just off Mulholland

Drive, the home where he would live for the next twenty-five years. In 1968, he paid $75,000 for it. In July 2016, it was put on the market for over $5 million, and Lady Gaga bought it later that year.

Why I Felt Bad

On December 4, 1971, while performing at Casino de Montreux in Switzerland, someone in the audience set off a flare that started a fire that burned down the casino and the band's equipment. Later during that same tour, at the Rainbow Theatre in London, while the band was packing up, a man named Trevor Howell came onstage and pushed Frank into the orchestra pit thirteen feet below.

Frank suffered serious fractures, injuries to his back, leg, and neck, and a crushed larynx. The damage to his larynx caused his voice to drop a third, the only somewhat positive result of the assault. His attacker got off easy. In January 1972, the *London Times* described the incident this way:

> *A man who attacked Frank Zappa, the pop group leader, because he thought Mr. Zappa was not giving value for money, was jailed for 12 months by Judge Rigg at the Central Criminal Court yesterday. Trevor Charles Howell, aged 24, a laborer, admitted maliciously inflicting grievous bodily harm on Mr. Zappa during a concert at the Rainbow Theatre, Finsbury Park, London. Mr. Howell was said to have run on to the stage and pushed Mr. Zappa, causing him to fracture a leg and cut his head. Mr. Zappa was in hospital for six weeks.*

Had I been there when the fire in Montreux happened, I doubt I would have been much help. Had I been there in London, I might now be the one in jail, and Howell would be worm food. But the Montreux disaster and the Rainbow Theatre assault had not yet happened as Frank was moving into his new home.

In 1968, I was living in Pomona, California, a town thirty-five miles east of Hollywood. Even though I'd visited Frank when he lived in the log cabin, my studies and part-time work, coupled with his new touring schedule, didn't allow us much time for visits after he moved to Woodrow Wilson Drive. Over the next few years, our paths would cross less frequently, but our friendship and brotherly bond remained intact.

Diploma Time

In May 1969, I had completed four years of undergraduate work at California State Polytechnic University in Pomona, and I was about to graduate with a bachelor's degree in history. I would be the only child in the original Zappa family to do that.

My father once said that he didn't think I had the ability to attend, let alone complete, college, so this was a pretty big achievement for me. In fact, I had even applied to several graduate schools, with an eye on one or maybe two more degrees.

I was interested in sociology at the time, and one of the best programs was at the University of Stockholm in Sweden. This is where Gunnar Myrdal, a Swedish economist, sociologist, and politician, taught from 1960 to 1967. He received a Nobel Prize in 1974 for his theory of money and economic fluctuations and the interdependence of economic, social, and institutional phenomena. Myrdal is best known in the United States for his book *An American Dilemma: The Negro Problem and Modern Democracy*, a study of race relations. The book has been credited with influencing the 1954 landmark US Supreme Court decision *Brown v. Board of Education*, which overturned *Plessy v. Ferguson*, the 1896 Supreme Court decision upholding state laws requiring racial segregation in public facilities under the doctrine of separate but equal.

In 1969, the University of Stockholm's program in sociology bore Myrdal's political and economic imprint, and I thought the mix of those disciplines was intriguing. I had dreams of becoming a college professor, and I thought a degree in sociology from the University of Stockholm would be good training. My dream was in the distance, but Stockholm was not. So I applied in the spring of 1969 and was accepted in July for the 1969–70 academic year. It was time to scramble.

The thought of uprooting life in California in exchange for the unknowns of life as a graduate student in Sweden was daunting. My wife, Marcia, would have to give up her job as head nurse at a California state hospital, a secure position that we would later wish she had somehow been able to keep. We would have to give up our inexpensive rental home, store what we wanted to keep, and find a garage for our cherry 1965 powder blue Ford Mustang. Anyone who has been faced with those kinds of decisions knows how stressful they can be.

Fortunately some friends from college had a garage that we could use for the car, and after selling off what we didn't want or couldn't keep, we packed what was left in the Mustang and pulled it into our friends' garage. Stage one of our excellent adventure had been completed.

2

Stockholm and the Potty Poster

When we celebrate ignorance, and make that the national standard of excellence, we embarrass ourselves.

—Frank Zappa

Stockholm, Sweden

After being accepted to the University of Stockholm, Marcia and I spent many frenetic days in July 1969 trying to figure out how to pay for the program and where we would live once we got to Stockholm—and asking ourselves what the hell I was thinking.

We managed to get a student loan that would cover the cost of the program and part of our living expenses, and we withdrew our savings to pay for the rest. The exchange rate from dollars to kronor was pretty good back then, so we worked out a budget that we hoped would see us through the first year. So many new things to consider and so many fears to overcome. We were excited about going, but we were nervous about how we'd deal with those issues.

In August 1969, we packed our bags and headed for LAX and the SAS flight. Neither of us had ever flown to Europe, so this was a big deal. The flight was about thirteen hours, and at the end of it, we were anxious to get off the plane and get our bearings. Looking out the plane's window as we descended onto the runway at Arlanda Airport in Stockholm, I was sure other passengers could hear the rumblings in my gut as the reality of what we were about to do was rapidly sinking in.

We first stayed in a youth hostel in Stockholm, but the next day, we went looking for an apartment. We were lucky to find a studio apartment on the island of Kungsholmen, across the causeway from the center of Stockholm. It was also near a stop on the Tunnelbana, Stockholm's subway line, giving me easy access to the university.

We moved in that afternoon and started unpacking, and Marcia made out a list of things for me to get at a neighborhood market. On the list, in addition to food, were beer and wine. We were going to celebrate that evening with Swedish meatballs and alcohol. So I went to the market and got as many of the items on the list that I could find, including the beer and wine. The beer was labeled *lättöl*, a word I didn't know at the time. And the wine was a Spanish rioja tinto. The beer and the wine were expensive by California standards because of the heavy taxes the Swedish government put on alcohol.

But regardless of the cost, we were going to enjoy our first night in Stockholm in modest but optimistic style.

After we finished unpacking, Marcia set the kitchen table with our dinner and drinks, and we got the party started. It was a great first night in our new home, except that we must have been so excited that, at least in my own case, the beer had no effect—I drank four of the six bottles and got no buzz. Marcia found the rioja drinkable, but she found that it stained her teeth a bit. We learned later that *lättöl* is used to designate a beer that contains no more than 2.25 percent alcohol by volume. No wonder I didn't get a buzz. And Marcia's rioja was rumored to be used for dyeing cloth.

Downtown Stockholm and Easy Rider

The center of Stockholm is called Hötorget (ho-tory-ett). When we were there in 1969 during the daytime, and weather permitting, the area was a fruit-and-vegetable market. On Sundays, it was a flea market. The Swedish concert hall, or Konserthuset, the Filmstaden Sergel multiscreen theaters, and the NK (Nordiska Kompaniet) department store are all within walking distance of the center. On our third day in Stockholm, we ventured downtown to see the city center, and one of the first shops we came across was a large record, poster, and memorabilia store. In its windows were posters of rock musicians. Among them was the famous one of Frank sitting on the toilet. Frank told me that he had been paid $1,500 to pose for that poster, and he later heard that the company selling it had made over $5 million from domestic and international sales.

A few nights later, we went to see *Easy Rider*, the 1969 film written by Peter Fonda, Dennis Hopper, and Terry Southern, about two bikers who travel through the American Southwest after selling a large score of cocaine. It was a film that explored the social issues and tensions in the United States in the 1960s. In the theater that night, there were several men who spoke English, as we picked up from their running commentary during the movie.

At first, it didn't seem all that unusual. Moviegoers in California and elsewhere in the United States are known for their rude and annoying chatter in theaters. But we were in Sweden, and it dawned on me that the quiet viewers were most likely Swedes.

After the show, I went up to two of the young men and asked how they liked the film. They spoke English, clearly the American version, not the British. I asked where they were from, but they just offered, "The States."

I said, "I'm from LA. Only been here a few days. How long have you guys been here?"

One answered, "Not long. What are you doing here?"

I told them, "I'm going to graduate school."

They just looked at me. The other one asked, "Were you in the military?"

I said, "I was in the Marine Corps. Went to Cuba during the missile crisis and then to Vietnam."

They quickly looked at each other and then started to move like they were going to leave. But before they could go, I asked, "Were you guys in the military?"

They didn't answer right away, but one eventually said, "Yeah, we served." But he quickly changed the subject and asked, "Do you know a cheap restaurant?"

I said, "We haven't been in Stockholm long enough to find one."

Before I could say anything else, one guy said to his friend, "Thanks anyway, man, but we gotta go."

Suddenly it dawned on me that they might have been deserters. I had mixed feelings about that. I was glad to be talking with other Americans but did not know how to handle the possibility that they might have run away from a significant responsibility. As bad as it was for so many others, either in legitimate protest against the war or in fear for their own safety, desertion during time of war is a serious offense.

But as I looked around, I saw other guys who had the same "stateside" appearance, a different look from the Swedish men in the lobby, and I came to the same conclusion about them. At the time, Stockholm was a favorite place for deserters, and a fairly large group of men had made their way to Sweden to avoid Vietnam. Their presence was a source of contention for the Swedes, who did not support America's involvement in Vietnam but didn't like the idea of these deserters living off the Swedish social welfare system.

Many years later, Bill Harris, who had become a successful Hollywood celebrity interviewer, was doing an interview with Dennis Hopper in a suite at the Four Seasons hotel in Los Angeles. Bill invited me to listen in.

When they finished the interview, Bill introduced me to Mr. Hopper, who immediately said he remembered meeting me, but he couldn't say from where.

He said, "Man, you look very familiar. Where did we meet?"

I said, "We've actually never met before."

He looked at me for a few seconds and then said, "No, man, we met somewhere. I just can't remember where or when. Did you ever live in Malibu?"

I said I had not but added, "I did, however, see *Easy Rider* in Stockholm, and if you were there on a promotional tour, you may have met guys who had deserted from their units to avoid going to Vietnam, and I may have looked like one of them."

He looked at me and said, "I hear you, man. That must have taken real courage."

I didn't have the heart to correct him again, so he went away thinking I was one of the deserters.

Deviant Behavior

One of my classes was in the sociology of deviant behavior. It focused on the different institutional interpretations of deviancy: how religion defined it, how the legal system defined it, and how the average Swede defined it. That was the frame of reference for the course, Swedish deviant behavior.

We learned how statistics were used to measure "deviance" from norms. We also got to experience deviance in action. In 1969, a sex education film called *Ur kärlekens språk* (*Language of Love*) was a box office hit throughout Sweden.

The film also caused uproar in Europe. In London's Trafalgar Square, some thirty thousand people gathered to protest in front of the movie theater showing it, calling the film pornography masquerading as a documentary on sex education. Duh!

US customs reportedly confiscated copies of the film, and it was labeled a sexploitation film. But that did not stop the Swedes or anybody else in Stockholm from watching it. And it was, as I recall, a pretty entertaining "how-to" film that we watched, pretending to be disengaged from the action scenes but enjoying every minute, since it was one of the course requirements.

Another course activity was a field trip to a pornographer's studio, where we saw the sets for, but no actors actually performing, the photo shoots that were published in printed books. We did see the end products of that enterprise, though: a series of four small hardcover photo books depicting graphic sexual positions in full color. They were called, for some strange reason, *Piff*, *Paff*, *Riff*, and *Ruff*. They were small enough to fit in a purse or a suit-coat pocket. They weren't as thick or as small as those little Red Ryder comic books from the 1950s, but they could be easily concealed for quick reference. I loved the enlightened Swedish approach to sex!

3

My Russian Holiday Adventure

*You can't be a real country unless you have
a beer and an airline—it helps if you have
some kind of football team, or some nuclear
weapons, but at the very least you need a beer.*

—Frank Zappa

Stockholm, Helsinki, St. Petersburg, and Moscow

With three months' worth of classes under my belt, I found that, much to my surprise, I liked studying abroad. I'd made friends with grad students from Australia, Holland, Germany, and Portugal. I felt at home in that international community and was open to new experiences. And a whole slew of them were about to kick in.

On Thursday night, December 18, 1969, Marcia and I, along with other students from the university, were invited to a cocktail party at the Russian Intourist office in Stockholm. In those days, Intourist was the Soviet tourism and travel agency that screened visitors before allowing them entry into the Soviet Union. We'd been thinking about going on a two-week tour of Leningrad and Moscow with students from the Russian language department, and the staff at Intourist had offered to give us the details of the trip. The Cold War was still sputtering along between the United States and the Soviet Union, but the Russian politburo was trying to attract Western tourists.

The Russian economy was teetering on the verge of collapse, and an infusion of Western currency, especially from tourism, could help. Students were exactly the kind of visitors they wanted. And while we didn't have to pay a lot to travel and stay in the Soviet Union, we certainly got what we paid for.

Our journey began on an overnight cruise ship, the HMS *Bore*, that had sleeper cabins. The ship took us into the Baltic Sea, up into the Gulf of Bothnia to Turku, Finland. The next morning, we got up refreshed and ready for the next part of the trip, a train ride from Turku to Helsinki. The temperature in Turku was about fifteen below, but we soon boarded a sleek, modern Finnish train that was nicely heated and had large, comfortable seats.

When we got to Helsinki, we got off the Finnish train and waited for our luggage so we could cross the tracks to board a Soviet train that would take us into St. Petersburg. Then we walked a short distance to the Soviet train station and saw an aging locomotive linked to ten wooden boxcars, complete with dirty windows and a chimney on top of each car. Our group was herded into the last car.

The car had wooden benches and wooden overhead racks for our bags. The chimney we'd seen from the outside was connected to an iron potbellied stove inside sitting next to a small bin of coal. The transformation was jarring. We realized we had just left the free world and the modern conveniences we took so much for granted and were now about to embark on a woefully out-of-date mode of transportation into what can only be described as a third world country.

We had been sitting on the wooden benches for about thirty minutes when several soldiers and two men in plain clothes came in and spoke Russian with our tour guide, a young man from the Intourist office named Bertil. When they finished, Bertil told us to take out our passports. He collected them and gave them to the plainclothes men, who then left the train. We didn't see our passports again until we got back to Helsinki almost two weeks later. The thought of traveling without documentation made me nervous, but what was even more disturbing was the fact that the Russian authorities were now able to research our identities. We were never told that we'd be under that kind of scrutiny when we signed on for the trip.

The train ride to St. Petersburg was a lot more uncomfortable than our ride from Turku to Helsinki, and we were all in a very bad mood after almost seven hours in transit across the vast wasteland between Finland and Russia. That area, we were told, was filled with landmines, and anyone trying to escape from Russia on foot across that terrain ran the risk of being blown up.

A Hilton Hotel It Wasn't

It was about eleven thirty at night when we got to St. Petersburg, where the temperature was thirty below zero. The youth hostel where we had reservations was closed. Or more specifically, the innkeeper was asleep, and she had to be awakened to let us in. She was angry that we were late, and since we were tired and sore from the long trip on wooden seats, it wasn't a good start to our visit to Mother Russia.

Each room had its own bath and toilet, so we were thankful for small comforts. Marcia decided to take a bath, so she turned on the water in the tub and came back into the bedroom to unpack. When she went back to get into the tub, the water was dark brown and smelled of iron oxide. The water from the tap in the sink was also rusty, as was the toilet water. We ended up letting the tub drain and using the tap water sparingly to wash our hands and faces before collapsing in bed.

The next morning at breakfast, we were told to wait until a group of West German tourists finished eating. Breakfast wasn't worth waiting for, though. By the time we got in to eat, we were served slices of thick, dark bread; hard cheese; strong black tea; hard-boiled eggs; and a substance they said was yogurt but smelled like very sour milk.

We found it curious that the Russians treated the Germans with such deference, when in the past two major world conflicts, one of Germany's main objectives was to invade and conquer Russian territory. Keeping one's enemies closer than one's friends must have been their strategy.

In St. Petersburg, we visited the Hermitage, the winter palace of the Russian monarchs until 1917, when the Russian revolutionaries stormed the palace and removed the last of the czarist rulers, Nicholas, and his wife and children. We were able to see the priceless collection of jewels, paintings, and furniture. One exhibit was an enormous malachite vase. I was standing near it, trying to see how the small pieces of malachite had been put together so intricately, and I made the mistake of trying to touch the vase. As I began to extend my arm, out of nowhere a viselike grip clamped down on my wrist and pulled me back. I turned to see a large, older woman in a smock who probably could have broken my wrist but instead just glared at me. I looked around and saw other large, older women in smocks who were clearly the babushka security force. For the rest of our time there, I kept my hands to myself.

After the Hermitage, we were taken to a Russian Orthodox church, where we witnessed a marriage ceremony. It was a strange ritual in an even stranger setting. The church had no seats, the building itself was in the shape of a cross, and the wedding party looked like they weren't having much fun going through the service.

As we watched the priest deliver the vows, our tour guide was explaining what was happening in a voice loud enough for the bride, groom, and wedding party to hear. All of a sudden, it seemed inappropriate for us to be there and even more so for our guide to be talking during the ceremony.

I stepped close to him and said, "Bertil, could you keep your voice down? You're being disrespectful."

He looked at me like I had just farted and stood quietly for a few seconds. Then he nodded and stopped talking.

Communists didn't care much for religion back then, especially if those who practiced were not party members. We quickly learned that we had very little free time that wasn't supervised and chaperoned. We saw what they wanted us to see and little else.

After our stay in St. Petersburg, we got on another train and headed for Moscow, but this time the seats weren't wooden, and the cars didn't rely on a coal-burning stove for heat. The trip was not uncomfortable, but it was boring. There wasn't much to see that time of year because of the heavy snowfall.

In the Heart of the Enemy's Camp

When we got to Moscow on December 29, it was forty below. We were picked up in cattle car buses that had no heat and were so cold that the windows were frozen...on the inside. They took us from the train station to a site about twenty miles from Moscow, one of the many Communist Youth Camp compounds built in the late 1950s to house Communist youth for one of the festivals the Soviets held annually to show the world how successful Communism was and how much the young people benefited from it.

The buildings were dilapidated, and the rooms, while grand in dimension, had uncomfortable beds covered with sheets thin from overuse and thick Soviet Army blankets. The furniture was worn and dirty and had a musty odor. There were a few broken windows covered with sheets of wood and tape. The temperature in the rooms was about fifty-five degrees during the day and even colder at night. There were communal showers and toilet stalls with no doors.

As was the case in St. Petersburg, our meals were served in an enormous hangar-like room that smelled of cabbage and strong black tea. I imagined that there were probably prisons in the United States with better accommodations. In an effort to offset our disappointment and frustration with the miserable accommodations, our tour guide told us that Moscow was going to be the best part of our trip. He said we were going to the Palace of Congresses in the Kremlin to hear the Red Army Chorus and then to the Bolshoi Theater on New Year's Eve to see *The Nutcracker*, performed by the Bolshoi Ballet Company. And after the show, we were scheduled to go to one of Moscow's best nightclubs, a place called the Blue Moon, to ring in the New Year with members from the Communist party.

But before we got to do any of that, our guide told us with great pride and enthusiasm that we would first have the privilege of seeing Lenin's Tomb, and then we would get to go to GUM, Moscow's version of a badly run, poorly stocked K-Mart.

Nose Trouble and Hands Up!

The day we got to visit Lenin's Tomb, it was bitterly fucking cold, unlike the day before, when it was just fucking cold. We started out by waiting in front of the youth hostel for the tram to take us to Red Square. One of the guys in our group did not have a scarf around his face like the rest of us, and we noticed that his cheeks and the tip of his nose were turning white. Just then, an old woman walking by stopped, looked at our friend, and said something to him in Russian.

Our friend gestured that he didn't understand, so the old woman touched her face and nose with her gloved hand. Our friend didn't get it and stupidly mocked her by doing the same thing. Bertil finally noticed what was going on and started walking toward us, asking what was happening. As our friend turned to look at Bertil, the old woman bent down and picked up a handful of snow. And when our friend turned back to face her, she tried to rub the snow on his face and nose.

He pulled away and swatted her hand. By then Bertil told him to stop that and said something to the old woman in Russian.

She nodded, said *da*, and walked away.

Bertil turned to our friend and said, "You should have let her rub the snow on your face. She was trying to save your nose by getting your circulation going. You need to do that yourself right now, or you risk frostbite."

Score one for Old World remedies.

Having lived most of my life in Southern California, the coldest weather I can remember was during a training exercise with the Marines in the Mojave Desert, when it got down to about twenty-nine degrees above zero at night. The extreme temperatures in Russia were panic inducing and downright scary, which was why I was wearing practically every piece of clothing I'd brought with me on the trip. I looked like the Pillsbury Doughboy.

When Lenin Was All the Rage

When the tram finally came, we got on and headed for Red Square. A half hour later, we arrived and saw a line of at least three hundred people waiting to get in to see Lenin's Tomb. Our immediate reaction was, "Hell no! We won't stand in line at those temperatures."

But Bertil said we wouldn't have to. He said we'd be going to the head of the line because we were Western tourists. That was supposed to impress us because, for the average Russian, getting a glimpse of a waxen corpse was the closest they would ever get to a Madame Tussauds wax museum experience, and we were expected to show our respect and appreciation for that special privilege.

As we approached the entrance to the tomb, Bertil told us to keep our hands in plain sight because the guards, large Russian soldiers with Kalashnikov rifles and unpleasant looks, didn't particularly care if our hands were cold. They wanted to see them—no ifs, ands, or buts.

But one student in our group from New Jersey prided himself on his rugged individualism and his all-American, can-do attitude. He was so tough that he wasn't even wearing an overcoat. He did have a few sweaters on beneath his sports coat, though, along with a big, woolly scarf, earmuffs, and a deerstalker cap. He was also wearing gloves, but his hands were hidden in the pockets of his sports coat. I was behind him, and as he reached the first of the (many) Russian guards, the guard signaled for the student to take his hands from his pockets.

The student ignored the guard and casually looked around to show he wasn't intimidated. The guard signaled to him again to remove his hands, but the student still ignored him. The guard then walked up to the student, towering over him by at least a foot, let his rifle hang loose on his shoulders, and put his face within inches of the student's face.

At that moment, our group watched with a mix of fear for our classmate and, for me at least, mild enjoyment at watching him get publicly spanked. Without saying a word, the soldier reached down, grabbed the student's wrists, and yanked his hands out of his pockets. Message received, action taken, and the line resumed moving. This was one more very real example of the control the Russian government had over behavior in what was still a very oppressive regime. It was also a good lesson in how not to behave like a jerk in the enemy's camp.

Once inside, we walked around a semicircle guarded by more Russian soldiers with rifles at the ready, and we got a peek at Vladimir I. Lenin's waxen figure. It didn't take long, and it wasn't very interesting, but it was what tourists were expected to do regardless of the weather. Nobody said any prayers, though. Praying in public was not needed. What was expected was strict observation of and devotion to the father of the Revolution.

Where K-Mart Got Their Idea for a Superstore

After our visit to the tomb, we got to see Russian commerce in action. We made our way to Russia's premier department store, GUM, which stands for "main universal store" in Russian, but for us, it stood for "Godawful Ugly Merchandise." But the best part was the way the Russian consumers bought that stuff. Here's the drill:

1. Choose your item from one line.
2. Move to the next line to pay for it.
3. Move to another line to pick it up.

Smooth, efficient, and fast. No, wait. That's McDonald's. GUM service was convoluted, slow, and rife with errors. But that was how they did things. You wanted stuff from GUM, you had to pay the price. Nobody in our group bought anything, though. We were only there for a mercifully short time, mainly to see commie commerce in action.

For our final adventure in Moscow, we were taken to the Palace of Congresses, a majestic auditorium where the Russian politburo met until 1991 and where we saw the Red Army Chorus perform Russian folk songs, including the rousing and thoroughly enjoyable "Kalinka." After that, we got back in the cattle cars and headed for the Bolshoi Theater to see *The Nutcracker*. The performance completely blew me away. The music was amazing, and the dancers were incredible.

After the ballet, Bertil told us, "When you get back to your rooms, be sure to rest up for the evening's festivities. I guarantee that you will have the best New Year's Eve celebration ever, starting with a sumptuous feast with more different kinds of vodka than you ever thought existed."

The Blue Moon Café was, as promised, a trendy, well-appointed, and well-managed hot spot for Communist party officials. We were greeted like honored guests and shown to our tables, and the food and liquor began to flow. Each table had an open bottle of vodka, champagne, and white and red wine, all waiting to be emptied. We took that responsibility seriously, and in short order, the empties were quickly and efficiently replaced.

The promise of the different kinds of vodka was no joke. There was one called hunter's vodka that was the color of bourbon and had an alcohol content high enough to power a tractor. Others were of varying alcoholic levels, color, and title, but as the evening wore on, they all blended together.

Along with the vodka, they also served Russian beer. The beer was the strongest I had ever drunk, but it served a useful purpose: it counterbalanced the effect of the vodka. What that meant was that the heavy drinkers in the crowd could down as much vodka as possible, wash it away with high-octane beer, and then hit the vodka again.

Did I mention that "washing away" was a euphemism for barfing? Well, it was, which was a shame because we were served a different meal for each of the time zones across Russia, and the food was actually quite good if you could keep it down. We started with beef, then chicken, then lamb, and then duck, but by the time we got to the next time zone's delicacy, I was doing my best to purge the vodka and the beer, along with whatever else was in my system, shoulder to shoulder with my commie hosts. Looking back, it was, as promised, the best part of our trip.

But by the next morning, we were all anxious to get back to Stockholm and a much-appreciated return to Western civilization. I missed the freedom the Swedish government afforded its citizens and visitors. I missed Swedish food and pastries. I even missed Swedish TV, even though I didn't understand all of what was said. And I missed having my passport.

4

How I Almost Became a Russian Spy

*Communism doesn't work, because
people like to own stuff.*

—Frank Zappa

Moscow and Stockholm

Before we left Moscow, we were told that we'd get our passports back when we got on the train to Finland. We learned later from one of the professors in the Russian language department that information on our passports had been carefully recorded and our identities thoroughly researched. I wasn't concerned about that at first, but the reality of that began to sink in as the next series of events unfolded.

Back in Stockholm, I started classes again, and we settled back into our routine. One afternoon about two weeks later, we got a call from a man named Victor (who pronounced it "Wicktor") who said he was from Intourist and wanted to know how we liked our trip to Russia. He asked if we'd like to join him for dinner downtown so we could talk about this in person. We had a policy to never turn down a free meal, so we met Victor at a fairly decent restaurant on Sveavagen, the main boulevard in downtown Stockholm.

Victor was a charming man who gave us the impression that he was really interested in what we had to say about our trip. That night we had a decent meal and some good wine, and Victor paid for a cab to take us home. We chalked up the evening to good public relations and went about our business the next day.

A week later, Victor called again and asked if we wanted to join him for pizza. As far as I'm concerned, the timing is always right for pizza, so we met Victor at a pizza place where students from the university hung out.

He bought the pizza and beer, and we talked some more about Russia. He wasn't pushy, nor did he say much about the motherland. So we made another mental checkmark on our ever-growing list of free meals and again went back to our day-to-day routine. For me, it was early up, a quick breakfast, onto the subway platform, and in class by 9:00 a.m. After class, I would stop at a corner kiosk, get a grilled *korv* (hot dog), and make my way to the library to do some research or maybe catch a quick nap. Marcia attended

Swedish language classes and then did grocery shopping or visited a museum or one of the stores in the center city. It was a fairly stress-free existence for both of us.

After another week or so, Victor asked if we'd like to see the movie *Anna Karenina*. Movies, pizza, and free dinners. The annuity from our trip to Russia was paying off. As we started to walk into the theater, he said he was coming too. That didn't seem all that unusual at first, but after the movie, he suggested we go for coffee, and we happily agreed.

As we were finishing up, Victor asked if we'd given any thought to ever going back to Russia. We said it wasn't high on our list because we couldn't afford it and because our experiences there didn't exactly make us want to plan a return visit any time soon.

Then Victor asked if we would be interested in going back, all expenses paid with first-class accommodations. He said Intourist would pick up the tab because they wanted people like us to come back to the West and tell our friends all the good things that we experienced.

He said, "Vee doan tink you got a goot impresshun of our country, and vee vant to make up for dat." He had a thick accent, that guy.

We're Getting Suspicious

We were thrown off guard by his offer. Our habit of taking advantage of anything offered at no charge was about to kick in, but Marcia asked when the trip would take place. Victor said we should go in the spring, when all of Russia would be in its glory. Marcia said we'd like to think it over and get back to him. Victor said that was okay, but he'd need to know soon in order to book the best travel arrangements.

We talked about Victor's offer with some of our Swedish friends. At first, our friends' reactions were reserved, which we interpreted as mild envy. I later realized that they knew what was going on. We, of course, didn't.

But when I told one of my professors the news, he reacted differently. He asked if we had asked Victor what we might have to do in return for this free vacation. He suggested that if Victor said that we wouldn't have to do anything, it might be worth considering. But if Victor said he wanted us to do anything at all in return for the trip, we were better off not going.

We called Victor and said we wanted to talk about the trip, and he said we should meet him at the Intourist office. When we got there, Victor took us into a small room with only a table and four chairs. Then he closed the door and positioned himself with his back to the door and us across the table from him. I think we were probably being filmed, but I didn't see a camera.

I started by saying that we were interested in going but we needed a few more details, so he said to ask away. I told him that the trip sounded too good to be true, and we didn't want to find out that we owed Intourist money.

He didn't respond immediately, but he did give us the kind of look that used-car salesmen give when they think they have a buyer for the only car on the lot that nobody else wants. When that didn't work, his demeanor suddenly morphed into that of a kindly older relative.

In soothing tones, he assured us that we were being much too cautious and that he was sorry he didn't make things clearer to begin with. He also told us that there would be no expense to us whatsoever, but if we wanted to repay his kindness, perhaps we could bring something with us on the trip to give to another Intourist official in Moscow.

I said, "Well, Victor, that all sounds wonderful, but we would like to give it a little more thought so we can plan our schedule. Can we get back to you in a day or so?"

He looked at us for a few seconds and probably decided against trying to convince us any further, because I think he was pretty confident that he had us hooked.

He said, "Vell, dat vood be fine."

The next morning Marcia and I went to the American embassy and asked to speak with someone about our meetings with Victor. We were told to take a seat and were offered coffee and pastry, but we declined. We were too nervous for the meeting to be anything but business.

We'd been sitting there for about forty-five minutes when a tall man with sandy brown hair asked us to come into his office. He introduced himself as an official in the public affairs section, which came as a bit of a disappointment since I didn't think our situation exactly fell into in the category of public affairs. If anything, it was something the defense attaché should've known about.

But we figured we had to start somewhere, so we told the official about our trip to Russia with the university and how Victor had contacted us when we came back. I told him about the dinners, the movie, and the offer for us to go back to Russia at no charge. I added that he wanted us to take something to an Intourist official in Moscow, which was why we were telling him the whole story.

When we finished, he asked if we felt threatened by Victor in any way, or if we were anxious about any repercussions from contact with Victor and Intourist. He said, "We know about Victor because he's made the same offer to other students in the past, although none of them got as far along in the process as you have."

He added, "That's Victor's job. He recruits students to go to Russia as couriers, but most students ignore him after the first contact."

The inference was that we weren't smart enough to figure out what he was trying to do.

He then said, "At this point, you don't have to worry about Victor anymore, and you should go about your business."

I asked, "How did you know about Victor, and why we shouldn't worry about him in the future?"

He said, "Actually, someone from the American embassy was aware of Victor's efforts to persuade you to return to Moscow, especially during the times he took you out. What you don't know is that after your last meeting at Intourist, Victor was recalled to Moscow."

He didn't offer any other explanation about that, and he didn't encourage any more discussion.

He said, "I want to thank you for being responsible American citizens. You don't need to worry about any further contact from Intourist or any Russian national here in Stockholm. Have a nice day, and good luck in school."

With that, we left his office and the American embassy.

It occurred to me that someone had been watching us every time we went out with Victor, and if we had gone back to Russia at Intourist's expense, we could've been in deep shit. We never heard from Victor again, and we never went anywhere near the Intourist office for the rest of our time in Stockholm.

After we returned to California, I told Frank about the incident. He laughed and said, "Well, Bobby, that should teach you something about commies. If you had fucked up and gone back with documents, you could have ended up in some prison in Siberia, or worse, in prison here. Wise up."

My brother: always the clear thinker and no mincer of words.

Back in the USSR

My winter adventure in Russia in 1970 is something I'll never forget. I'm glad I got to go there at a time when Communism's failure was apparent and I was able to see how that affected the Russian people.

Years later, in 1988, I went back to Moscow as a member of a US government trade mission with Samuel Pierce, the secretary of Housing and Urban Development, during the early stages of glasnost. "Glasnost" was the term used beginning in 1986 to describe an increased openness and transparency in the Soviet government. Mikhail Gorbachev led this movement in an effort to improve social, economic, and political life in Russia.

It was also a time when corruption in the Communist party was at its peak and social unrest was building. Censorship and freedom of information were under constant scrutiny and remained a cornerstone of the Soviet system of control. In addition to the social reforms initiated under glasnost, Gorbachev also sought help from Western governments to rebuild Russia's crumbling, long-neglected infrastructure.

At the time, I worked for a division of McGraw-Hill that published detailed information about computers and communication equipment. I managed the division's office in Lausanne, Switzerland, and I was asked to present our products at a meeting of the politburo in Moscow at the Palace of Congresses, along with thirteen other men from American companies seeking to do business with the Soviets.

Information about computer technology was desperately needed back then, but not as much as the Russians needed bathroom fixtures and plumbing, caulking material to repair crumbling concrete sidewalks and walls, and systems designed to improve productivity, such as managing and processing inventory.

When I went to Moscow, I stayed in a hotel not far from Red Square. It had a huge atrium, similar to those in hotels designed by the architect John Portman. The name of the hotel (which is probably long gone by now) was the Mezhdunayrodniya, which was Russian for "international." It was a poor imitation of anything Portman designed. My room was a sad blend of the worst furniture you'd find a Motel 6, coupled with the Soviet's idea of Western comfort.

I saw two single beds and one nightstand in between them with a lamp, a dresser, and a television with a twenty-eight-inch screen set inside a wooden cabinet big enough to conceal a small man and all the latest commie electronic bugging equipment. I had the feeling that I was being watched every moment in my room. At one point, I even knocked on the cabinet and asked if there was anyone in there and, if so, did he want to come out and have a drink with me. Nobody took me up on my offer, though.

In the mornings, for exercise before our meetings, I would walk from the hotel up to Red Square. One morning I happened to notice that the cars parked along the street had no windshield wipers. None of them. When I got back to the hotel, I asked the concierge about that, and he said that car owners removed the wipers each night to avoid having them stolen. I asked if that was because they were too expensive to replace.

He said, "No, it's because there aren't any available to be purchased."

With my curiosity piqued, I asked, "Why is that?"

He said, "The last five-year plan did not include windshield wipers."

His answer spoke volumes about why Communism was a failure. Instead of allowing market forces to determine product demand, the rigid Soviet system decided for consumers what would be available, like it or not. The Russian government today has moved away from the five-year-plan model but maintains control over how citizens behave in what is still a secretive and oppressive regime.

5

Back to Los Angeles

Definition of rock journalism: people who can't write, doing interviews with people who can't think, in order to prepare articles for people who can't read.

—FRANK ZAPPA

Stockholm, Sweden, and Hollywood, California

IN MAY 1970, we learned that Marcia was pregnant with our son, Jason. We decided to return to Los Angeles at the end of the term in Sweden to regroup and restart our lives where we'd left off the year before. I had earned a Swedish research diploma in sociology at Stockholm University and was planning to continue with another degree, with the goal of teaching. Life, of course, had other ideas about that.

When we returned to the States, Bill Harris put us up at his Venice Beach apartment until we got settled. His place was one block in from the ocean, and it was a great way to ease back into the California lifestyle. Marcia was growing rounder by the day, and I began to worry about the tasks ahead.

In 1970, Ronald Reagan had been elected governor of California, and under his administration, the economy was headed for a recession. Jobs were already getting scarce. My job hunt was grueling and often fruitless.

Meanwhile, in 1970, Frank was busy touring and establishing the Mothers of Invention brand worldwide. He had formed a new group that included Aynsley Dunbar, George Duke, Ian Underwood, Jeff Simmons, and three members of the Turtles, Jim Pons, Mark Volman, and Howard Kaylan. This was also the year Frank released *Chunga's Revenge*, followed by the soundtrack to the movie *200 Motels* in 1971. That film featured the Mothers, the Royal Philharmonic Orchestra, Ringo Starr, Theodore Bikel, and Keith Moon.

After the log cabin, Frank moved into his house on Woodrow Wilson Drive in the Hollywood Hills. It had seven bedrooms and six bathrooms. There was a basement that Frank turned into a workspace with a Movieola editing machine, a vault for tapes and film, and walls covered with Zappa license plates and other fan memorabilia from all over the world. He also began construction of one of the most sophisticated recording studios in Hollywood, the Utility Muffin Research Kitchen (UMRK), which became his sanctuary and source of inspiration.

While Frank was enjoying more professional and financial success, he was too deeply engrossed in his projects to pay much attention to me or anyone else in our family. That wasn't as much an issue for me as it was for Mom, Dad, Carl, and my sister, Candy. There didn't seem to be enough time in his day to maintain contact with us, which I think he regretted toward the end of his life.

Money, Honey

During that period, as I was struggling to find work, I had given up on the idea of going back to graduate school, and I was constantly worried about making ends meet. After three months of searching, I finally got a job with Pacific Finance, a division of Transamerica Corporation.

Pacific Finance was in the business of making loans to individuals and families who did not qualify for bank loans. As a trainee, one of my responsibilities was debt collection, which involved actual collection of money from people who were in default in their loan payments. I hated that part of the job. Actually I hated everything about the business, but it was work, and we needed the money.

The office was in South Central Los Angeles, at the time a dangerous and hostile part of Los Angeles's vast urban sprawl. Strip malls with barbershops, liquor stores, and other random businesses dotted the area where, in August 1965, the Watts riots had taken place—six days of mayhem and destruction in which thirty-four people died and $40 million in property damage was done. I did not like that job, nor did I like how the people who borrowed money from the company were treated. But you do what you have to do to survive. There are limits, though, and I reached mine after only three months.

Another trainee, a black man and Vietnam army veteran named Joey, and I were partners in the collections part of the business. One day, we had to call on an overdue account. The borrower was 120 days past due, and we were supposed to either get some form of payment or bring in the person to renegotiate the loan…at a higher interest rate. It was an unpleasant task, to say the least, and one that could have led to disaster given the circumstances.

We got into Joey's car headed for Watts and began looking for our collection's address. Joey was familiar with the area, and we found the house sooner than I expected. We parked in front of a run-down California bungalow and walked up to the front door. Joey took the lead, explaining that he could probably talk to the borrower more easily than I could, since we both figured the person was black and probably wouldn't take kindly to a white guy asking him for money.

When we got to the front door, Joey knocked—a little too loudly, I thought—but there was no answer. He knocked loudly again and asked for the person to come to the door. Still no answer. I breathed a sigh of relief and said we'd done our best and would have to come back another time.

Joey said with surprising conviction, "Shit, man. I know he inside, and we gots to get him to come out."

So he gave it one more try, really banging on the door. That was when I got nervous. This time, the door flew open, and we came face-to-face with a very large black man wearing a wife beater T-shirt and holding a double-barreled shotgun.

After surviving three years in the Marine Corps, including a brief tour in Vietnam preceded by a three-month stint as part of the Cuban missile blockade, I did not want to get blown apart on a street in Watts. Washing dishes, sweeping floors, or doing anything else besides collecting bills was now looking pretty good as a career path.

And to make sure I might live to exercise that option, I turned and began walking back to Joey's car, hoping that either the shotgun wasn't loaded or that Joey got the first volley so I could run screaming down the street like a little girl being chased by a giant bunny rabbit.

As I reached the car, I hadn't heard the shotgun go off yet, but as I turned, I saw Joey shaking his finger in the guy's face, again saying with conviction, "Man, you got to live up to your financial obligations. We [meaning Pacific Finance] can help you work out your problem, but you gots to come to the office to do that."

Amazingly the guy seemed to be buying that load of crap and had even lowered his shotgun as he listened to Joey talk pure corporate trash. Finally, when Joey was done giving the guy the pitch, they actually shook hands, and I heard the guy promise he would come to the office tomorrow. Whether he did or not, I would never know, because when we got back to the office, I quit right on the spot.

My boss wasn't all that surprised, and he didn't try to convince me to stay. So that ended my brief career as a moneylender and bill collector. When I told Marcia the story, she wasn't happy that I'd quit since we had a baby on the way, but she agreed that it was probably better than waiting for the next time when I might confront a heavily armed delinquent borrower.

When I told Frank about it, he laughed and asked, "What the fuck were you doing working for that company in the first place?"

I said, "That was the only job available at the time."

And he said, "Bullshit. Find another one."

Frank had strong opinions about things, like self-actualization and independence. In some ways, he was a lot more conservative than I was. He had been—and still was—an employer, and he had high expectations of the musicians he hired.

He expected me to get my act together and quit screwing around. He wasn't so much unforgiving as he was simply demanding. He worked harder than any other rock and roll musician of that era, and when he wasn't doing that, he was composing serious music. So giving anything less than 100 percent was, to him, simply unacceptable. And he expected me to do the same.

After quitting Pacific Finance, I went to work for a janitorial service. The hours were 7:00 p.m. till 3:00 a.m., which meant I could still go to the beach when I wasn't looking for another job.

One day Frank called to say that he knew a magazine publisher who was looking for a "stringer," a freelance journalist to attend and write about rock concerts in the Los Angeles area. Her name was Pauline Riveli, and she was the founder, publisher, and editor of Jazz Press, Inc., the parent company of *Jazz & Pop* magazine.

I contacted her, and she offered me the job on a per-article basis. She also gave me a press card, which allowed me backstage access at rock shows. I attended a few and wrote some articles about them, but not all of my stories made it into print. Still, those were really cool times, and publishing was slowly becoming my career path. Or so I hoped.

6

When Working in Publishing Was Cool

So many books, so little time.

—FRANK ZAPPA

South Central Los Angeles

WHILE I WAS working for the janitorial service, I was also busy making contact with anyone who might have a lead on a real job. While networking like crazy, I contacted a former college professor, who said he knew someone who might be able to help. He introduced me to a young man who was a field sales representative for the college division at the McGraw-Hill Book Company in New York. His sales territory included six four-year colleges and three junior colleges in the Upland and San Bernardino area. His job was to meet with professors to tell them about the new textbooks McGraw-Hill was publishing for the courses they taught. The texts he plugged covered many disciplines: math, science, engineering, social science, humanities, business, and nursing. It sounded like something I could do, and I was very interested.

We met one day for an interview over lunch in a nice restaurant, and we discussed the duties, benefits, and career opportunities associated with working for one of the largest publishing companies in the world. I was even more interested in the job when he told me that it came with a company car, expense account, and two months off in the summer.

I tried not to get my hopes up, but when I got a call from the regional manager for Southern California, who asked if I could come to San Francisco for a second interview, I began to think my time with bowl brushes and Windex was about to end. The opportunity couldn't have come at a better time. Jason was about ready to join our family, and having a job with health benefits was a big plus.

So one Monday in November 1970, I got on a PSA jet at LAX and flew to San Francisco for the interview. The regional manager met me at the airport, and we drove into San Francisco to the Clift Hotel, one of the best in the city. He dropped me off and said he'd be by later to pick me up for a dinner meeting with the general manager for the Western region. Intense pressure was about to be applied, I thought.

At six thirty, the regional manager picked me up, and we drove to the Cliff House, a really cool restaurant overlooking the Pacific.

The general manager and two other men were waiting for us, and it looked like I was going to be dancing pretty fast if I wanted the job. The interview started with drinks. I had a Dos Equis while the others had scotch, vodka, and bourbon. Two of the men smoked. In those days, smoking in restaurants was allowed. So it was to be drinks, smoking, and light banter before the inquisition began.

But the inquisition never got off the ground. I began to realize that I wasn't going to be asked job-related questions. I was going to be judged for what I soon learned was my "hail fellow, well met" quotient. Could I be one of the guys? Could I hold my liquor? Did I chew with my mouth open? Did I like or know any fart jokes? What sports teams did I follow? I had a second beer and decided to do my best to be one of the guys.

One small obstacle, though, was the fact that I had been in the Marine Corps. I learned that none of the others had served in the military, so my time in the Corps was met with mixed reactions. The older guys said my service was appreciated, while the younger guys made excuses for why they couldn't or didn't serve. Part of that was their shared belief that not having served was not that big a deal. Or that serving in the military was for guys who were unable to weasel out of that obligation, especially during the Vietnam War. I got an uneasy feeling about that but knew enough to keep my mouth shut.

After a manly dinner of steaks, baked potatoes, creamed corn, rolls, and more drinks, we ended the evening at around eleven. The general manager pulled me aside and said he liked what he saw and that the next day he wanted me to visit his office in Novato, California, a town about an hour north of San Francisco. He wanted me to meet the support staff for the field reps and to talk further about my thoughts on the company and the job itself. The regional manager would pick me up at 8:00 a.m. and get me there for the meeting. After that, I had a flight back to LAX in the afternoon.

At 8:00 a.m. sharp, the regional manager drove up, and we headed for Novato. We got to the office a little after nine. We went to the cafeteria for coffee and to discuss how the support staff worked. I was very impressed with their cafeteria. It had hot food for employee breakfasts, lots of hot coffee, a bright, airy room, and clean tables. It was clear that McGraw-Hill was a big, prosperous company that really needed me.

The rest of the visit went well. I met some very nice people, and I even got to go back to the cafeteria for lunch. Lots of eating and drinking happened in this job, I thought. After lunch I met with the general manager, who told me that the person who'd interviewed me first in Southern California was being promoted to an editorial position in San Francisco and that his territory was going to be open. Was I interested in taking his place?

I said I definitely was, and then he handed me an employment contract that spelled out the job, salary, benefits, and other things that didn't matter at that moment. What did matter was that I now had my first official, real, big-boy job in a field where I thought I could prosper.

Getting Started

When I told Frank about my new job, he had one bit of advice. He said, "Show up for work on a regular basis, don't fuck up too much, and they'll make you president one day."

When I told him about the reaction to my service in the Marines, he said, "Look, you want the job, right?"

"Of course."

He looked at me for a moment and then said, "So what the fuck do you care what those guys think?"

And once again, he was the voice of reason in the midst of a sea of babble. My predecessor left for his new job in San Francisco, but not before turning over his files, expense account book, and company car.

I was now part of another big organization. After having learned the military procedures in the Marines, the rules governing McGraw-Hill employees were a piece of cake. Now all I had to do was learn about the books and the courses they were written for and put them together with professors in the different schools in my territory. It sounded easy at first, but the amount of information to master was enormous.

I began the learning process with reams of product information about the books that were sent to me from the New York office. That was the mysterious and elevated place where the real business of textbook publishing was performed. I wondered about the people who made it all happen there and whether one day I might be part of that. But I was getting ahead of myself, so I put that thought aside and hunkered down to learn the basics of the products and the business.

Meanwhile Marcia was getting ready to deliver, and because of the timing (early January 1971), I was able to stay close to home. In fact, early one morning she told me that her water had broken and we needed to get to the hospital immediately. That was going to be a challenge since the hospital where our son was to be born was in West Covina, California, a forty-five-minute ride from North Hollywood, where we lived at the time.

I quickly bundled Marcia into the car and headed east on the Hollywood Freeway, hoping to get there before our son decided to make his entrance. Luck was on our side. We got to the hospital in about an hour and got Marcia into the OR and me into the fathers' waiting room.

Before we left, I called Bill Harris to let him know we were on the move, and not long after, he showed up at the hospital to join me in the waiting room. As good friends do at times like these, Bill brought a bottle of Jack Daniel's and a six-pack of Coke. We didn't know how long it would take for Marcia to deliver, so he came prepared for a long siege. As it turned out, it was indeed a long one, almost nine hours.

Finally the doctor came out to say that he'd had to perform a C-section and that mother and son were doing fine. But by then, Bill and I had finished the bottle of Jack Daniel's, and I was pretty well oiled. The doctor misinterpreted my reaction, which was not much of one at all, by asking a nurse to bring him an ammonia ampul, which he quickly broke under my nose. I guess he thought my lack of reaction was an indication I was in shock, so he wanted to snap me out of whatever he thought I was in. Word of caution, men: try not to get an ammonia ampul cracked under your nose after drinking Jack Daniel's and Coke, because a kick in the balls would be easier to take. The ammonia and the bourbon were a potent mix that sobered me up and also made me want to barf.

I kept it together and eventually got to see Marcia, but not our son. I was told that I wouldn't be able to do that until the following day. It was hospital policy. So I left for home, sober and now mildly terrified at the responsibilities ahead.

Getting Real

After three days in the hospital recovering from her C-section, Marcia and Jason came home to our apartment in North Hollywood. The fact that I was now responsible for a child along with a wife and all that went along with being an adult meant my learning curve was going to be steep. As a newly minted father and a brand-new sales rep for McGraw-Hill, I was determined to justify the confidence the company had placed in me and to ensure our family's well being… and, as Frank advised, to not fuck up.

So I set out one day to visit my first college campus and make my very first sales call. I brought with me all the good news I had gotten about McGraw-Hill textbooks. I wanted to prove that I could deliver the goods and make the sale. I felt and must have looked like a missionary: short-sleeved white shirt, skinny black tie, pocket protector, and all manner of zeal for the written word.

My first call was with a professor in the English department at a junior college in San Bernardino. I had a new style manual that was intended to compete with Strunk and White's *The Elements of Style*. The first edition of that book was published in 1918 and revised in 1959, and in 2011, *Time* magazine named it one of the one hundred best and most influential books written in English.

The book I was promoting, as I quickly learned, had very little chance of replacing Strunk and White, but ignorance was bliss in this case. After proudly introducing myself to the professor, who looked at me like he probably did at the freshmen he clearly detested, I started my pitch.

After only a few words, he asked, "What's in it for me?"

I'm not known for quick assessments of ambiguous situations, but in this instance I immediately got his point. I also knew that nothing short of a toaster oven or maybe a bottle or two of wine might help change his mind. I responded by telling him that his students would benefit, but he cut me off and said he had class in a few minutes. When I had something "better" to offer, though, I was to be sure to come back.

I thought, "What an asshole!"

That was my introduction to the dark side of higher education: a few greedy, self-important, and petty instructors whose idea of dealing with sales reps for textbook publishers was to see how much they could squeeze out in a bribe. But not every professor I met was that way.

In the Midst of Greatness

Later in my career, when I was the acquisitions editor for the physics program, I went to MIT. My goal was to find a professor who might be interested in writing a quantum mechanics text, a hot topic in physics. Anyway, while I was wandering around the halls at MIT, I remembered Dr. Paul Samuelson, the McGraw-Hill author of the best-selling introductory economics text.

I had seen him receive his Nobel Prize in Stockholm in 1970 when I was there as a graduate student. The statement for his award said that "he has done more than any other contemporary economist to raise the level of scientific analysis in economic theory." And the *New York Times* called him "the foremost academic economist of the 20th century." Impressive credentials indeed, but I thought it worth at least stopping by his office to pay my respects since we had Stockholm and McGraw-Hill in common.

I found his office and thought that, if he was not there, I'd leave a business card and a brief note. But incredibly, he was there, his office door was open, and I saw him sitting at his desk reading some papers. Dr. Samuelson was the picture of an Ivy League professor: distinguished looking, white hair, glasses, tweed sports coat, and bow tie.

I knocked timidly, and he looked up and smiled. That threw me off completely. I gave him my name and said I was from McGraw-Hill. I started to tell him why I was at MIT, but he cut me off by standing up and asking me to come in. He extended his hand, and after I shook it, he asked me to have a seat.

Here was a world-famous Nobel laureate, tenured MIT full professor, and one of McGraw-Hill's best-selling authors sitting across from me, and I realized I was in the midst of greatness unlike any other I had ever known. He asked me why I was visiting MIT, and I told him about my author acquisition search. He said he knew a few professors in the physics department and would be happy to give me their names and even contact them for an interview. I thanked him and said I would very much appreciate that.

Then I mentioned, somewhat awkwardly, that I had seen him receive his Nobel Prize in Stockholm, and his face lit up. He asked how that came to be, and I told him about being in graduate school at the University of Stockholm. He stopped me and asked if I had lunch plans. It was about twelve thirty, and I thought it would be an honor to take Dr. Samuelson to lunch. I didn't know of any restaurants in

Cambridge, but he anticipated that. He said he'd like me to be his guest at the MIT faculty club.

His offer completely blew me away. He wanted to take *me* to lunch. At the MIT faculty club! In those days, there were no cell phones that could take pictures, but if there had been, I would have taken dozens—lots of Dr. Samuelson, his office, and the stately faculty club replete with fireplace and deer antlers over the hearth, along with me looking stunned but enjoying every second.

He asked, "What were you doing in Stockholm?"

I said, "Studying social psychology, specifically deviant behavior."

He paused a moment and then said, "Well, that must have prepared you for the publishing world." And he chuckled at his own observation.

I was curious about that remark, so I said, "I hope your experiences with McGraw-Hill have been nothing but positive."

He only smiled and nodded.

We talked for about an hour over lunch, and when we finished, I thanked him for his hospitality.

He said, "I appreciate you stopping by, and I hope you find the next McGraw-Hill physics author here at MIT."

With that, we shook hands, and I left him at the faculty club.

It has been one of my fondest memories of my entire time with McGraw-Hill. With great authority comes even greater modesty. Many professors never achieve either, but Dr. Samuelson had both.

7

New York, the Second Time Around

> *If you're going to deal with reality, you're going to have to make one big discovery: reality is something that belongs to you as an individual. If you wanna grow up, which most people don't, the thing to do is take responsibility for your own reality and deal with it on your own terms.*
>
> —Frank Zappa

Midtown Manhattan

After working as a sales rep in Los Angeles for almost four years, I was contacted in October 1974 about a job opening in the New York office. It was for the physics editor's position. In those days, in McGraw-Hill's college text publishing division, there were two types of editors. One was called "basic book editor," which was a bit misleading because editors in those positions were usually content specialists who could actually edit copy. In the science publishing field, the basic book editor for physics would have to have a degree in physics and know how to write for the average college student buying textbooks. Editors in that position were considered "real" editors.

The other type of editor was called the "sponsoring or acquisitions editor," and that job did not require a specialized degree. But it did require prior field sales experience and a significant amount of the "hail fellow, well met" personality. Schmoozing was an added bonus, as was a fairly high tolerance for alcohol.

Evidently I had developed a fair number of those traits; I had also not been arrested while on the job and had actually made a few large sales, all of which put me in the running for the sponsoring editor's job in physics. The thought of a big promotion and a move to New York was exhilarating, and I wanted the job badly.

As the year wore on, the lure of working in New York for the largest publishing company on the planet began to occupy my thoughts. I also experienced "approach-avoidance conflict." This describes a decision-making situation that has both positive and negative ramifications. An example of this would be someone making a decision about a job that has financial gain and prestige but also a great deal of stress and long hours. In making a decision, the person must assess whether the positive aspects outweigh the negative. This was my dilemma.

I was growing discontent with the Los Angeles lifestyle because in those days, one had to have a chocolate-brown Mercedes, a house with a pool, a housekeeper, and a six-figure income to be part of the Los Angeles scene. And it didn't hurt if you knew an actor or some other celebrity or were related to one. To be fair, being Frank's brother didn't hurt. Often when I'd meet with a professor on campus to talk about books, I'd be asked if I was related to Frank. If I thought it would help land a book adoption, I'd admit to that. If not, I'd ask who Frank was, which usually ended our meeting. Call me shallow, but this was business. It wasn't personal.

Often if I said I was related to Frank, a professor would ask if I could get him or her tickets to one of Frank's shows in exchange for a sale. Sometimes that request was a joke; other times it was a dead-serious bribe solicitation. I learned that college professors on the whole are honorable, intelligent, and dedicated, but some are just assholes, like in any other profession.

Learning how to deal with many different professors was the best training ground for the sponsoring editor's job, because the sole purpose of that assignment was to convince professors to write a textbook for the program being sponsored, and McGraw-Hill wasn't the only textbook publisher in the business. There was archrival Prentice-Hall and a host of lesser players like Wadsworth, Houghton-Mifflin, Macmillan, Brooks-Cole, and many others, even less notable. So the trick to being a successful acquisitions editor was in knowing how to read professors. The training ground as a sales rep was ideal for that, and I thought I was ready to make a move to the big time.

How My Decision Was Made

One June day in 1975, when Frank was off the road, he called and asked me to pick him up at his house. He said he was hungry and wanted to get an In-N-Out Burger. There was an In-N-Out Burger on Lankershim Boulevard, not far from my first apartment in North Hollywood on Emelita Street. In-N-Out burgers and their fries were great because they were cooked right when you ordered them. The buns were toasted, and the meat was fresh, as were the sliced tomatoes and onions topped with shredded lettuce, mayo, and, if requested, mustard. But I digress…

Anyway, I picked up Frank, and we headed for the In-N-Out Burger drive-through. I began to tell him about the possibility of moving to New York to work for McGraw-Hill, and he said, "That's great, Bobby. Get the fuck out of LA and grow up."

I said, "I've been growing up for a while now."

He said, "But you won't be as grown up as you would be if you can cut it in New York." He also said, "Your first time in New York [with Frank at the Garrick in 1967] was a test run, and you should have learned from that. Don't fuck it up this time."

And that was when I knew I wanted the job and would jump at the chance, if it was offered. In June 1975, the job offer came through, and that was the start of a major life-altering event for me.

By the mid-1970s, Frank was regrouping and moving in new directions. The major setbacks of 1971 (the Montreux fire and the Rainbow Theatre attack) were receding as he recovered physically and artistically. During that decade, he produced the albums *Apostrophe* (1974), *Roxy & Elsewhere* (1974), *One Size Fits All* (1975), and *Bongo Fury* (1975) with Don Vliet, a.k.a. Captain Beefheart. He was by then widely known as a serious composer and recording artist as well as a technical wizard in his studio.

I admired his ability to multitask with such ferocious dedication and intensity. If I had only one tenth of his drive, I knew I'd make it in the Big Apple, big time.

And So It Came to Pass

In late July 1975, I flew to New York to meet with the publisher for the science group. That interview went well enough for the job to be offered and accepted on the spot. The next step was to sell my house in North Hollywood, find another one in New Jersey, pack up, move, unpack, and hit the track running. And I had to accomplish all that by the end of August.

Looking back on those events and how they were accomplished, I marvel at the resilience of the human body, because the stress was overwhelming. If I'd thought I was grown up in Los Angeles, the move to New York put a whole new spin on that phase of my life. Frank was right. If I could cut it in New York, I'd really start growing up. And so I did.

8

Publish or Perish

Everybody believes in something, and everybody, by virtue of the fact that they believe in something, uses that something to support their own existence.

—Frank Zappa

Ridgewood, New Jersey

THE FIRST STAGE of the transition to our new home in Ridgewood, New Jersey, from North Hollywood, California, was completed in late August 1975. My early childhood experiences with the constant upheaval of moving came flooding back, but not necessarily in a bad way. Moving across the country was more daunting for my wife, Marcia, and probably also for our four-year-old son, Jason. I suspect my can-do attitude (or my lack of sensitivity to their fears and concerns) helped them adjust faster. But in reality, I was scared to death about the move.

I didn't know what to expect as a new editor. I had an office on the twenty-seventh floor of the McGraw-Hill building at 1221 Avenue of the Americas, along with a secretary, new job-related tasks to master, and a whole new set of business behavior and protocols to learn in order to succeed…and not get fired. Getting fired was now an ever-present possibility for anyone who failed to live up to the demands of the job.

There were many days when I regretted leaving my life in California, the lack of supervision I enjoyed as a salesman, and the low stress that came with the job. In New York, there was the bull's-eye-on-your-back feeling, the constant fear that at some point somebody would be doing things behind the scenes to undermine your credibility in an effort to take over your job. That happened to me early in my tenure as the physics editor.

How I Almost Lost My Job

It happened this way. A woman (Sondra) who had been hired as the basic book editor for physics, who had a degree in physics and some prior editing experience, made a pitch to my immediate boss that she had better qualifications than I did for my job. I learned that she questioned my business sense and whether I knew enough about physics to actually determine if a manuscript was worth publishing.

She was a bit sketchy about her personal hygiene, had the fashion sense of a Roller Derby queen, and gave the impression that she was on her way to the top, everything and everybody in her way be damned. Not that there's anything wrong with ambition, but in those days, that kind of aggressive approach was not a widely accepted business trait for a woman, especially in the male-dominated world of publishing. But the woman we both reported to was also ambitious, and she favored the woman who wanted my job. It was the first major challenge I faced, and I wasn't sure how to handle it.

Things went from bad to worse as Sondra kept pointing out my lack of knowledge about physics and said she should be given the chance to prove herself in my job. If that happened, I would be out on the street. Worse yet, I would have to scramble to find another job, with McGraw-Hill or not. It was a really difficult situation, and it caused me to question my own abilities.

One day, my boss, Charlene, editor in chief for science and mathematics, called me in to her office and said, "Bob, I don't think things are working out for you in the editorial part of the business. You don't know enough about physics to compete with editors from other companies to sign manuscripts. So I'm recommending that you go back to a field sales job, if one is available in this area. You will be relieved of your editor's position effective tomorrow."

I was stunned but managed to say, "That not fair, Charlene. I've only been here for six months—"

But she interrupted me and said, "You should have been able to master the job by now. And frankly, you don't seem ready to do acquisitions. I think you were brought in too soon."

I didn't have a response to that because I was too shocked to speak.

She added, "You can come in tomorrow and clean out your desk. I'll see you then to explain your next steps."

So I left her office, assuming I would be out of work before I had a chance to actually learn how to do the job. I was afraid to tell Marcia, so I didn't. I spent that evening at home, worrying about what I had done by uprooting her and Jason. I was angry with myself for thinking I could compete in the big leagues. That night I didn't sleep well.

The next day, I went to work, prepared for the worst. I got to my office at eight and began to go through my desk, sorting out things I would take or leave, but I got the sense that nothing had changed. I mean, nobody else in the office gave me the impression that he or she knew I faced impending doom. There were no awkward silences when I met someone in the hall and no sympathetic glances from the secretaries. In fact, when I went down to Charlene's office at nine, my boss wasn't at her desk. When I went by again at ten, she still wasn't there.

At eleven, I was called down to corporate personnel. I figured that was where I'd take the hit, come back, clear out my desk, go home with my tail between my legs, and give Marcia the bad news. But when I got to personnel, I met with a friendly woman, Mrs. Rosenberg, who asked me to have a seat.

She inquired, "How are you doing? How do you like working in New York?" She then added, "And how do you find working for McGraw-Hill?"

Her questions caught me off guard, but they also put me at ease. Was this the way they fired guys in the big leagues, making them feel good first and then kicking them in the balls?

I responded quickly and with as much enthusiasm as I could muster. "Mrs. Rosenberg, I love working in New York, and I'm thrilled to be an editor in the best book publishing company in the world. But frankly, I'm terrified at the prospect of being fired before I can prove myself in the job."

Mrs. Rosenberg looked at me for a few seconds, smiled, and said, "You don't need to worry about losing your job, but you do need to ask for help from other more experienced editors."

She was either very good at reading me or had gotten some direction from someone in our division about me trying to do too much on my own and not allowing the veteran editors to help me. I was stunned. I just looked at her, thinking that maybe I still had my job. And as it turned out, I did!

Then she added, "Charlene is no longer with the company, but a new editor in chief will be appointed in a day or two."

I wanted to ask why my boss had tried to fire me, but she anticipated my thought. She said, "What you need to do now is go back to your division and start working more closely with more senior editors to learn the ropes. I think you'll be a good editor one day, so take this opportunity to prove me right."

The impact of what she'd just said had not fully sunk in when she added, "And by the way, there will also be an opening for a new basic book editor in physics starting tomorrow."

When I looked at her after she said that, I thought I saw a slight grin on her face. Things are not always what they seem. For what it's worth, the old-boy network was on my side that day, which also meant that the two women who did their best to get rid of me did themselves no favors.

Whatever Happened to "Class"?

Over the years, educational book publishing in New York City has become less of an intellectual pursuit and more of a profit-driven business. When I worked for McGraw-Hill's college division, though, the company was the premier publisher of some of the most influential and scholarly textbooks ever written. Of course, MIT professor Paul Samuelson, the Nobel laureate in economics whose economics textbook was the leading text for decades, was one. Harvard professor and researcher Edward M. Purcell and Cal Tech professor Richard P. Feynman, both Nobel laureates in physics, were also authors published by McGraw-Hill.

The list of exceptional intellectuals was long and distinguished in the company's heyday. But the scavenging of corporations for obscene profit, the elimination of jobs, and the ridiculous price increases for textbooks have turned once highly sought-after careers and the companies that offered them into run-of-the-mill competitive job factories. Numbers-driven editorial acquisitions foster mediocre textbooks that contribute to the dumbing down of our educational system. The only saving grace might be that perhaps textbook publishers today have yet to figure out how to outsource jobs. Or given what's being sold today, maybe they already have.

9

Frank and Smothers Visit McGraw-Hill

"I don't want to write a book, but I'm going to do it anyway...one of the reasons for doing this is the proliferation of stupid books (in several different languages) that purport to be about me. I thought there ought to be at least one, somewhere, that had real stuff in it."

—FRANK ZAPPA, *THE REAL FRANK ZAPPA BOOK*

New York City, Avenue of the Americas

BY LATE OCTOBER 1977, I had been working for McGraw-Hill in New York for almost two years. That was also the month Frank did a series of shows at the Palladium in New York City. He once said that he loved playing for New York audiences because they were always wildly enthusiastic. On the downside, he said the New York City theater unions were just about the worst of all US cities. But he liked the Palladium, and his shows there were usually sold out, especially his Halloween extravaganzas. More on that in a minute.

Frank came to New York on the Thursday before his first show and checked into his hotel, the plush Mayfair on the Upper East Side. Back then, Sirio Maccioni's legendary Le Cirque restaurant at the Mayfair Hotel was Frank's favorite place to eat. He did so often, and in the process, he got to know and then became friends with Maccioni.

Anyway, someone in Frank's manager's office in Los Angeles called me at McGraw-Hill to say that Frank wanted to see me. They told me to call him at the Mayfair, which I did. And when we connected, we agreed to meet for lunch on Friday. He said he wanted to see my office and what it was like in big-time publishing.

I reminded him that I was in big-time "educational" publishing, which was not as glamorous or financially rewarding as publishing blockbuster novels that became blockbuster movies. He said that didn't matter. He just wanted to see me in my office to determine if I was actually making it in the rough-and-tumble world of words on paper.

So on Friday at around twelve thirty, Frank and his bodyguard Smothers pulled up in front of the Forty-Ninth Street entrance to the McGraw-Hill building. They got out of their town car and walked into the lobby, leaving their driver waiting at the curb until they returned. Smothers was wearing his trademark *judogi (the jacket he wears when doing martial arts)*, black belt, and Levi's. Frank had on bellbottom ball huggers and a T-shirt under a chenille bathrobe.

In those days, there was no security, no barriers to entry, and nobody to question who or why they were there. There was, however, an information desk, and Frank asked the man sitting there how to get to the twenty-seventh floor. The attendant asked whom they were going to see, and Frank gave him my name. The man called my office, and my secretary answered. The attendant told her that I had two visitors, and she told him to send them up. I went to the elevator bank on our floor and waited. When the doors opened, Frank and Smothers stepped out. Frank saw me, laughed, and gave me a big hug. I could see the people in the elevator straining to figure out what Frank Zappa was doing at McGraw-Hill.

Then Smothers gave me a big hug and a kiss on the cheek and asked where the bathroom was.

Frank said, "Okay, Bobby, let's see your office."

I said, "It's not much."

And he said, "I don't care."

I took Frank down the hall and past the secretaries sitting outside each editor's office until we came to mine. My secretary was an older woman who had worked for McGraw-Hill for many years. I suspected she was assigned to me with instructions to keep me from making too many mistakes.

When I introduced her to Frank, he was very polite and asked her if she thought I was doing a good job. She said it was maybe too early to tell, which Frank thought was a reasonable assessment.

I took him into my office, which was not very big. It faced another building across Forty-Eighth Street, but it had a view of the

Hudson River if you pressed your face against the window, looked to the right, and squinted.

Smothers found us and was talking with my secretary when Frank said, "Let's eat. Smothers is starving."

I asked, "Where do you want to go for lunch?"

He asked, "Do you have a cafeteria?"

McGraw-Hill had a great employee cafeteria in the basement, and Frank said that was where he wanted to go, so we headed for the elevators.

When we got on, a few others were in the elevator, and they stood in what could best be described as stunned silence while looking at Frank and Smothers.

The cafeteria was brightly lit, with rows of fluorescent lights, a vast sea of tables and chairs, and a fairly large gathering of employees eating, talking, or reading newspapers. We started through the line to get food. Frank said it reminded him of a scene in *Soylent Green*, the science-fiction movie about a murder investigation in a future world decimated by pollution, overpopulation, depleted resources, and dying oceans because of the greenhouse effect. Much of the population survives on processed food rations, including a mysterious substance known as "soylent green."

I told Frank I ate there often but had never come across any anything overly processed. He ignored me and got black coffee, a corn muffin, and some mashed potatoes. Not exactly well balanced, but that was what he liked.

Meantime, Smothers was selecting one item from every food group. They were ahead of me, so when it came time to pay, Frank said to the cashier it was on me. Then they both walked through and began looking for seats. My big brother must have figured I could afford it, and it felt good to treat them both.

We sat down and ate lunch as the rest of the room stared at us. We talked about our kids along with working in New York, living in New Jersey, and commuting. Frank talked about the show, his annual Halloween extravaganza, and asked me to be there.

I asked if I could bring some friends, and he said to call Harriet Delsener, Ron Delsener's sister, for tickets. Ron was the promoter who arranged New York City shows for Frank and just about every other rock artist. I knew Harriet from previous phone conversations and would be able to get the tickets I needed. I also knew my friends would love the show.

Frank's Halloween show was performed on Sunday, October 30. Marcia and I went with three other couples. We had seats not far from the stage, with a great view of the band. The Palladium was packed, and the marijuana smoke was approaching smog level. When Frank and the band came onstage, the crowd roared.

Frank said hello to the crowd, as he always did, but this time he added, "And tonight we have a few special people in the audience—my brother Bobby; his wife, Marcia; and a few of his New Jersey friends. Stand up, Bobby, and let them see you."

I stood, I waved, and the crowd cheered. Then I looked at Frank, and he laughed. I laughed. Then I sat down. Less than fifteen seconds of fame but a lifetime of memories were crammed into that brief exposure. After that, Frank introduced the band members, and they started playing. I think Frank liked introducing me at shows, to let fans know he had a family.

Similarly, at Dweezil's Halloween show on October 30, 2016, at the Beacon Theater on the Upper West Side of Manhattan, he did the same thing. He told the audience, "There's a special guest here tonight, Frank Zappa's brother and my uncle Bobby. Stand up, Bobby."

I stood, I waved, and the crowd cheered. And then I waved to Dweezil. He laughed, I laughed, and I sat down. I think Dweezil wanted his audience to know the same thing that Frank did, that he had family—a sane, ordinary, supportive family.

10

Mamma Zappa Goes to Mamma Leone's

My mother...is a devout Catholic, so who can tell what she really thinks about what I do or the things I say? I feel if you live life in the pursuit of "certification" from your parents, you're making a big mistake. The sooner you can say, "Okay, they're them and I'm me, and let's make the best of it," the better off you're going to be.

—Frank Zappa, *The Real Frank Zappa Book*

"Rose Marie and Francis Zappa in the 1950s."

Mamma Leone's in 1977

AFTER DOING HIS shows in New York in 1977, Frank called me and said he was going to arrange for Mom and Carl to visit Marcia, Jason, and me in New Jersey. He knew our mother would like that kind of royal treatment. He also said he'd arrange for a limo to take us into the city for dinner at Mamma Leone's, a restaurant in Manhattan's theater district. It remained a tourist destination for years until the building was sold in 1994 to make way for condos.

FRANKIE & BOBBY: THE REST OF OUR STORY

Louisa Leone founded her restaurant in 1906. By 1977, it had become a food factory with eleven dining rooms and 1,250 seats, serving almost seven hundred thousand meals a year. It's been estimated that over the decades, more than 18 million people ate there. It was gaudy, noisy, and, in those days, smoke filled. One restaurant reviewer compared it to an army mess hall, only not as good. Our mamma wanted to go there because she had heard about it on the news in Los Angeles, and I think she figured, "How bad can it be if that many people eat there each year?"

The story goes that Enrico Caruso first talked Luisa Leone into opening Mamma's in 1906 in the family's living room on West Thirty-Fourth Street. On opening night, Caruso brought so many friends that many had to sit on wine cases to eat their fifty-cent meals. Years later, after the restaurant had relocated to the theater district, Will Rogers was a faithful customer, as was W. C. Fields. In 1954, Harry S. Truman returned a 1929 vintage Dom Perignon to the kitchen because it was from the first year of the Depression. In 1955, President Eisenhower gave Gene Leone, who succeeded his mother as boss, a personal lesson in how to cook a steak. That recipe set the restaurant's standard. In 1960, Elizabeth Taylor was denied entrance to the dining room because she was wearing slacks, so she had to eat in the lounge. Mom was thrilled to be there!

Mom was then in her eighties but was still able to get around without too much difficulty. With Carl to help her, the trip east and back to Los Angeles would be an adventure they would long remember. I was there at Newark Airport to meet them, and I could tell they were a bit anxious about their trip. I lightened the mood, collected their bags, and headed to our home in Ridgewood, New

Jersey, where they could relax and begin to enjoy their visit. After our dad died, Mom didn't do too much, so this trip was a big event for her.

Rose Marie Zappa was a quiet woman and definitely old school when it came to her kids. She was a wonderful mother and a good cook, and she was proud of each of us, especially Frank, not just for the success he enjoyed as a musician but because he remembered her on special occasions and because above all he made her laugh. Mom and Candy were very close, and she relied on Carl now that Dad was gone. And I know she was happy to see me settled in our new home in New Jersey and employed by McGraw-Hill.

Frank arranged for us to be picked up in Ridgewood, taken to Mamma Leone's, and then be driven around Manhattan so Mom and Carl could see the city. When the day came for our trip, a stretch limo pulled up. Our driver said he would first take us to the restaurant and would wait until we finished eating.

He also said, "When you're done eating, just come outside, and I'll be waiting. Then I'll take you on a city tour before taking you back to New Jersey."

The drive into Manhattan was Mom's first big thrill. Crossing the George Washington Bridge for the first time can be an awesome experience, and for Mom and Carl, it certainly was. We went down the Henry Hudson Parkway (a.k.a. the West Side Highway) and got off at Forty-Second Street. From there, we cut across to Ninth Avenue and then to Mamma Leone's.

When we got out of the limo and went into the restaurant, I could see Mom's excitement building. She had never been in a restaurant like Mamma Leone's, and neither had the rest of us. We were mesmerized by the size of the place, the number of people eating, and the energy it generated. Simply going into the restaurant was a thrill. I gave our name to the maître d', and surprisingly, we were seated right away.

The menu was large, but we easily made our choice: pasta with meat sauce or meatballs all around. We ordered our meals and began the classic out-of-towner's ritual: people watching. Mom, Carl, Marcia, Jason, and I took in the sights, sounds, and aromas of a night that would become a cherished memory for all of us.

After we finished eating, I paid with the cash Frank had given me, and we went outside. Mom asked if the dinner was expensive. I told her that it wasn't all that much, and Frank had given me more than enough to cover it. I think she liked that a lot, knowing that Frank was taking care of us. We found our driver and got into the limo, ready for the guided tour.

We first headed north and then east to the Avenue of the Americas. The first place we drove past was the McGraw-Hill building at 1221, where my office was. Mom and Carl were impressed. Our driver then took us around Columbus Circle and up Central Park West, past the West Side's most expensive apartment buildings: the Dakota, the Langham, the San Remo, the Kenilworth, and the Beresford.

We also passed the Museum of Natural History. At Seventy-Ninth, we turned left and then south on Columbus Avenue, heading downtown toward Greenwich Village. When we got to the Village, the first landmark I pointed out was the Garrick Theater. I told Mom and Carl a little about Frank's shows there and about my time with him. We then went farther south to Wall Street and the Battery. It was a grand tour complete with running commentary by our driver, one more memory for Mom and Carl.

In the End

In January 2004, eleven years after Frank's death, our mother, Rose Marie Zappa, passed away. She had been in declining health for some time and was by then in a convalescent hospital. In spite of the stress from the loss of her husband and firstborn son, she still managed to live to the age of ninety-one. My sister, Candy, and brother Carl were with her when she died. I was in New Jersey when it happened, but Marcia and I left for Los Angeles a few days later.

When Marcia, Jason, and I arrived at Mom's wake in North Hollywood, we were asked to wait in a separate room with Candy and her daughters, Eva and Julie; my brother Carl; and my half sister, Ann. We were told that Frank's wife, Gail, had requested that she and Frank's children, Ahmet, Diva, Moon, and Dweezil, be allowed to view Mom without having us in the room with them. No explanation was given, so we were forced to wait our turn. The only thing we could think of was that Gail did not want her children "exposed" to Frank's original family.

11

Frank, Smothers, and Bobby in New Orleans

Classical musicians go to the conservatories.
Rock 'n' roll musicians go to the garages.

—FRANK ZAPPA

Let's Eat Some More!

ON MONDAY, OCTOBER 20, 1981, I was on the last leg of a business trip for McGraw-Hill that put me in New Orleans in the early afternoon. I got my luggage, flagged a taxi, and headed out of the Louis Armstrong International Airport for the French Quarter. As we exited the airport road, I saw a billboard that showed Frank's picture with the announcement that he and the Mothers would be playing at the Saenger Performing Arts Center that night.

When we got to the Quarter, the driver dropped me off at the Monteleone Hotel on Royal Street a few blocks away from the heart of the city. I unpacked, took a quick shower, and then called Frank's manager's office in Los Angeles to find out where he was staying. They told me he was at the Royal Sonesta Hotel on Bourbon Street, so I got dressed and went looking for him.

I found the Royal Sonesta, went into the lobby, and looked for a house phone. I knew they wouldn't give me his room number, but I could get through to him on the phone. I found one and picked it up, but just as I did, I felt a large hand on top of my head. It turned me around, and when I did an about-face, I was looking at Smothers's chest.

John Smothers is very large and very intimidating, and he was Frank's all-time best bodyguard. He picked me up in a bear hug and almost squeezed the air out of my lungs, asking, "Hey, Bobby, what the fuck you doing here?"

I gasped, "I'm here to see the show and eat some oysters."

Smothers laughed and said, "Come on. We'll go upstairs."

And we did. He took me to a two-bedroom suite overlooking Bourbon Street.

Smothers said, "Take a load off, Bobby. Frank should be out in a few minutes."

Smothers then went into his bedroom, and I turned on the TV. By then it was about four thirty, and I was getting hungry. I didn't know what Frank and Smothers had planned for dinner, but I thought we could grab something together. There are many great restaurants on Bourbon Street, and I was thinking about gumbo, fried oysters, and cold Budweiser beer.

A little while later, while I was watching TV, at around five o'clock, Frank came out of his bedroom. When he saw me, he laughed and asked, "Where did you come from?"

"Detroit."

He laughed again and asked, "Do you want to see the show tonight?"

I said, "Of course, but I'm meeting with three coworkers from McGraw-Hill."

He added, "No problem. Bring them along." Then Frank called out to Smothers, "Let's eat!"

Smothers was there in a flash, and as we were about to leave, an attractive blond woman came out of Frank's bedroom and joined us. Frank may have told me her name, but it didn't register. I knew better than to start a background check, because I figured I'd never see her again. But she was pretty, and with her blond hair and Frank's inky black locks, they were a pretty cool-looking couple.

Frank said he was really hungry, so we took the path of least resistance. We walked across the street to a chain restaurant, but I don't remember which one. There were several early diners, mostly tourists and generally older folks.

Frank didn't draw much attention in that crowd, which I knew he liked. He did not like being interrupted between mouthfuls to talk with fans. He probably didn't like being interrupted that way at home either, but that's another story.

Anyway, Frank and I ordered burgers, fries, and beer, and the blonde ordered some fried fish dish. Smothers ordered pretty much everything else on the menu.

Frank and I started talking about this tour. He said, "I'll be coming to New York to play the Palladium at the end of the month. If you want tickets, call my office or Ron Delsener."

I said I'd love to see him in the city, and then he asked about Marcia and Jason. I asked about Moon and Dweezil. He said they were doing great. Then our food came, and things got quiet except for the chewing. It was almost six, and Frank needed to get to the venue for the sound check before the show.

The burger and fries were pretty good, as I recall—maybe not In-N-Out Burger good, but still. As we quietly ate, I noticed Smothers slowly down put his fork, which meant that either he had to go to the bathroom or something was about go very, very wrong. Wrong it appeared to be, because Smothers reached behind his head for the snap baton that was clipped inside the collar of his *judogi*. I was sitting to his right, and I saw his eyes dart above me as three men approached the table.

I looked at Frank and saw he was watching Smothers too. He had stopped eating, but the blonde, oblivious to the drama about to unfold, continued eating. I hate it when mealtime gets interrupted, too, but I really hate it if the interruption involves a bar brawl or, in this case, possibly early-bird-dinner fisticuffs. I sat there waiting for something to happen, and when it did, it was like letting air out of a balloon.

One of the guys standing behind me tapped me on the shoulder and asked, "Hey, Bobby, is that you?"

I turned around to see my old high-school friend Armando Bustos and two other guys I didn't know.

I said, "Hey, Armando, what's going on?"

And just like that, Smothers and Frank resumed eating, the blonde barely looked up, and Armando and I had a brief exchange that ended with him and his friends apologizing for bothering us. Dinnertime drama was averted.

12

Frank Plays the Saenger Auditorium in New Orleans

For the record, folks: I never took a shit onstage, and the closest I ever came to eating shit anywhere was at a Holiday Inn buffet in Fayetteville, North Carolina, in 1973.

—FRANK ZAPPA

New Orleans

AFTER DINNER, FRANK, the blonde, and Smothers went back to the Royal Sonesta before going to the Saenger for the sound check and to get ready for the concert. I went back to the

Monteleone to call my friends to tell them about going to the show. They were in New Orleans for the same meeting I was. Two of them, Jack Farnsworth and Bill Willey, had been to one of Frank's other shows in New York, so they knew what to expect. The third person, Roger Howell, had never seen Frank onstage, so it was going to be either a rude awakening or hopefully his first of many more shows to come.

I arranged to meet them at the Saenger Auditorium's stage door. I wasn't sure what Frank was going to do about their seats, and I hoped we'd be able to sit together. When we got backstage and in the room where the band was resting before the show, I said hello to the band members, and Frank said hello to my friends. He told them that they had seats in the audience, and Smothers then gave them three tickets.

Since he didn't have a ticket for me, I knew what Frank wanted me to do. He wanted me to sit onstage during the entire performance. He'd done that before, and it may have been his way of reminding me that I should have stayed with him after the Garrick Theater days so I could have been a fixture onstage, along with the amps and instruments. But those days were long gone, and even though he knew it, I think he still needed to let me know what I was missing.

When it was time for the band to go on, they left the room and walked unceremoniously onstage to pick up their instruments. By then the audience was clapping and cheering. But when Frank came out, the crowd went wild. He strutted onstage, picked up his guitar, put the strap over his shoulder, and began waving at the audience. The more he waved, the louder they screamed.

Frank always introduced the band members before and after each show, and that night was no exception. With each introduction, the crowd thundered their appreciation for each musician.

When he was done introducing the band, Frank said, laughing, "And tonight we have a special guest, my brother Bobby." I had been sitting on the sidelines on top of an amp when he said, "Bobby, come out here and take a bow."

I didn't expect that, although he had done it before, once in New York at the Palladium and again at Rutgers University.

Don't Mess With Smothers, College Boy: A Digression

The Rutgers concert was the show I went to with my son, Jason, and John Wing, the thirteen-year-old son of a McGraw-Hill coworker. When John, Jason, and I got to the Rutgers auditorium, we went to a side door, where a burly football-player type was standing guard. I told him that I was there as Frank's guest, and he snorted and said I had to buy tickets like everybody else. I gave him my name and asked if he could let Frank or someone in the band know I was there. And he said again that we had to buy tickets.

I was getting pissed but didn't want to cause a scene with my son and John there, and I was about to give in and buy the tickets when the door opened and Smothers appeared. When he saw me, he pushed the door guard aside with one arm and pulled me inside, along with Jason and John. I looked back and saw Smothers glaring at the door guard, who, by then, was back at his post, trying to look official.

Smothers took us backstage to see Frank and the band. Frank hugged Jason and me and shook hands with John. We talked a bit. Then Frank said it was show time, and the band got up and started filing out. Frank said we would be sitting onstage with the band, which must have thrilled Jason and John, but I expected to end up with a headache from the volume.

We followed the band and Frank onstage and found a place to sit stage right. Frank said hello to the audience and introduced the band members and then me. I came out onstage, and as always seemed to happen, the crowd went wild. It never ceased to amuse me that people I did not or ever would know felt it necessary to applaud my presence, meaningless as it was.

Anyway, the show got started, and the band was in rare form. From where we sat, I could see the side door where we'd come in, and out of the corner of my eye, I saw it open as the guard let a young man enter. I didn't think anything of it until I saw him approach the side of the stage where we were sitting. He had a camera in his hands and was about to climb up onstage when out of nowhere, Smothers jumped in front of him with his snap baton extended.

He yelled at the fan, "Get the fuck out of here!"

Smothers was so quick and so menacing that I nearly pooped myself on the kid's behalf. Jason and John just thought it was cool. The kid may not have realized it, but he was dangerously close to getting knocked unconscious, which would have been okay, except it would have interrupted the show.

I've said it before, and it's worth repeating: Smothers was the best bodyguard Frank ever had. Now back to New Orleans.

There's Bobby…Again

As the band was getting ready to play, Frank decided it was time to give the audience some comic relief. He knew how much I disliked crowds and being brought out in front of them, but he did it there at the Saenger Auditorium anyway. He told the crowd that he wanted to introduce his "little brother Bobby."

So I got down off the amp and walked out onstage. Frank came over and gently pushed me toward the front of the stage, laughing all the while. He liked to nudge me like that. He thought that was funny.

Anyway, as I got to the front of the stage, and as the fans were yelling, laughing, and generally going crazy at the idea that Frank even had a brother, let alone one without long hair, a young woman came up to the stage and threw a pair of panties at my feet. More loud noise, jeers, and applause erupted. Nothing quite like having thousands of people cheering when a pair of panties is thrown at you onstage! But even more bizarre is the fact that somebody actually did that. Frank told me to pick up the panties and take them to the side. As I did that, the volume in the audience was incredible. I felt like I had just scored the winning touchdown in a Super Bowl game or the last basket before the buzzer.

One can only guess what was going through the minds of the guys, or even the girls, as I picked up the dainty undergarment, carefully avoiding any hint that I was aroused or that there was anything that might have triggered my gag reflex. Actually I thought it was disgusting, but for Frank, it was his way of using me as a prop to add color to his show. To everyone watching, I was just Bobby, the suave, panty-picking, amp-sitting stagehand.

The New Orleans show, Rutgers University, and the Palladium—these are all great memories that will be with me for the rest of my days.

Then the shit hit the fan.

13

Why Can't I See My Brother?

It's better to have something to remember than anything to regret.

—Frank Zappa

"This photo was taken circa 1987 in Frank's basement. It was one of the few times before his death that we were able to meet in person."

Los Angeles, California

IN SEPTEMBER 1993, I decided it was time to see Frank in person. We had spoken only a few times by phone since he told me he had been diagnosed with prostate cancer. I remember that first call vividly.

FRANKIE & BOBBY: THE REST OF OUR STORY

It was about seven o'clock East Coast time when I answered the phone, and it was Frank. He sounded tired when he began to speak. As I listened, he started by asking, "Hey, Bobby, how you doing?" I replied, "I'm okay, but you sound tired."

There was a pause. Then he said in a shaky voice, "I want to tell you something before you read about it or hear about it on TV. I have prostate cancer."

I froze. I did not know what to say. Anyone who has gotten that same disturbing news knows the awful feeling that it creates: fear for the person who was diagnosed, fear about the expense involved in treating the disease, and fear that the treatments won't be successful.

I finally said, "Wow, that's some shitty news. How'd you find out?"

Frank hesitated and then said, "One day when I was in the studio, I went to take a piss but couldn't. The pain was so bad I nearly fainted." He went on, "After I couldn't piss, Gail took me to the ER in Santa Monica, and the first thing they did was stick a catheter up my dick and hang a piss bag on my hip."

Once that was done, Frank said, he could urinate without the pain and pressure he'd first experienced. But further testing was needed. His doctor had to determine how serious his condition was and how they would treat him. When his symptoms first appeared, his doctor may have checked his prostate-specific antigen (PSA), a test that looks for markers in the blood that may be a sign of prostate cancer.

That began a series of events that, in the end, failed to bring about a successful outcome to his battle. Back in the 1990s, treatment for prostate cancer included radiation, chemotherapy, and surgery. Removal of the prostate gland was then a risky procedure with negative consequences, incontinence and impotence being the most common.

During the phone call, after he regained his composure, Frank said, I'm not gonna have surgery, because if I do, I'll lose my *creative juices*.

That reaction was uncharacteristic of him, but I got the impression that he was being defiant in the face of a serious health crisis. I asked, "What do your doctors say about surgery?"

He replied, "We're not there yet, but I don't want anything to interfere with my work."

I asked, "What makes you think surgery would do that? Where did you get that idea?"

He answered, "Gail and I talked about it, and we agreed that I'm not going to do anything that radical."

After several doctor's visits, and with his prognosis uncertain, he opted for radiation treatments. Before he started them, Gail became his health-care advocate. Frank said that one of the first things she did was sprinkle salt on the doorjambs in their house. She told him that was her way of keeping evil spirits at bay. I never knew if she was serious about that or if she was just so distraught that she was going to try anything to cope with the problem. I also never knew if the salt was kosher or just plain iodized. But I did know that Frank had bigger issues than evil spirits to confront and that competent medical treatment was needed immediately.

Cancer Treatments

In 1970, the test to detect prostate cancer was developed by Norman Yang, one of the scientists who identified prostate-specific antigen (PSA), a substance that only the prostate releases into the blood. They found that a man's PSA level is like a thermometer reading. A sudden rise likely indicates that something is wrong. It's not always cancer, however. A high PSA reading can also be caused by swelling of the prostate that comes with old age. But the test can indicate cancer often enough that it can be a signal to perform more tests, usually a biopsy.

It's not known if Frank's initial medical evaluation included a PSA test. It's also likely that his initial discomfort, which was the first indication of a serious problem, would have alerted his doctors to a look for a variety of diagnoses. But further testing was needed, and once it began, he was, as they say, "in the health-care system."

My Visit to Los Angeles to See Frank

Each of the many times I called Frank's house after that first phone call, Gail told me that Frank was either asleep or having some kind of therapy and to try again. When I'd call back later, I got similar off-putting responses. After so many fruitless attempts, I was worried that I might not get a chance to actually see him, so I told my boss that I was going to take one of my vacation weeks to go to Los Angeles. Jason was in school, and Marcia was working, so I went alone. Bill Harris came through again and offered me his guesthouse for the week.

On a Sunday, I flew to LAX, rented a car, drove to Bill's place in Hollywood, and got settled. The next thing I did was to call Frank. Gail answered, and I told her I was in Los Angeles and wanted to come over to see him. She said he was feeling sick and couldn't see me then but to call on Monday.

My next call was to my mother. I told her I would be coming to see her, and I asked if there was anything I could bring for dinner. She said she would really like an apple pie from Marie Callender's, a restaurant and bakery in Toluca Lake, a town not far from her place in Valley Village. After I got the pie, I stopped at Ralph's Market to stock up on basics because I knew that Mom and Carl didn't always have access to a car to go shopping.

With the groceries and apple pie in hand, I drove to the duplex Frank had purchased for our parents and where Carl also lived with Mom now that Dad was gone. I hadn't seen Mom or Carl in about a year, and neither of them had aged well. They hadn't seen Frank since he began his cancer treatments, and Mom asked if I could take them to see him. I told her I would do that and said we would bring Candy too. Mom liked that, even though I knew that seeing him would be stressful for us all and especially her.

What's the Reason?

For the week I was in Los Angeles to see Frank, I called his house two or three times a day but was never given the green light to visit or talk with him on the phone. Toward the end of my stay, with Mom and Carl waiting anxiously for the chance to see him, I thought we should simply go to his house and demand an audience. But having had difficult experiences in the past with Gail, and given the prospect of disappointing Mom and Carl, I delayed taking that step.

I regret it to this day, because years later, I learned from Moon that she thought Frank never even knew I had called, let alone that I was in Los Angeles. That made me angry. I was angry that Frank didn't know I was trying to see him, and I was angry with myself for not taking more direct action.

But anyone who knew what Frank's home life was like knew how difficult it could be. I was also angry with Frank. Why didn't he ask Gail about me? Or did he? And if so, what was he told? Why didn't he try to call me in New Jersey? Would he have then insisted or at least asked if I could come to see him? Or maybe it was something as simple as him not wanting me to see him in his worsening condition. I also learned that Frank did have regular visitors, musicians and friends who came to see him even when he was at his worst. Why were they allowed and I wasn't?

So many questions and so few answers.

Maybe This Is Why

In the Tuesday, July 12, 2016, *New York Times* Science section, there was an article on page D-4 titled "When Abuse Is Psychological," by Abbey Ellin. The article describes research on emotional abuse conducted at the University of Massachusetts, Amherst, by Dr. Lisa Fontes. In her research, Dr. Fontes called the kind of abuse she was studying "coercive control." She described it as "a pattern of behavior that some people…employ to dominate their partners. Coercive control describes an ongoing and multipronged strategy, with tactics that [may] include manipulation, humiliation, isolation, financial abuse, [and/or] stalking."

Since Gail's death in October 2015, articles written about her praised her for fighting anyone who, in her mind, tried to usurp Frank's musical legacy. Oddly, her son Dweezil was collateral damage in her mission. He has been negatively affected by those efforts, resulting in legal barriers to his performances of his father's music. In other articles, journalists uncovered and reported on Gail's alleged financial mismanagement, litigation failures costing millions, and directives embedded in the Zappa Family Trust document that defy logic.

In Frank's final days, he may have experienced coercive control that probably kept him from seeing his mother and siblings.

So many questions and so few answers.

One writer speculated that some of Gail's actions might be interpreted as payback for Frank's philandering. Although Facebook is not normally considered a reliable information source, posts from Frank's fans have reached the same conclusions. In the final analysis, though, we will never know what efforts were actually made on his behalf to prolong his life. That makes it all the more difficult to accept his untimely death.

14

Frank's Death and Its Aftermath

I don't want to spend my life explaining myself. Either you get it or you don't.

—Frank Zappa

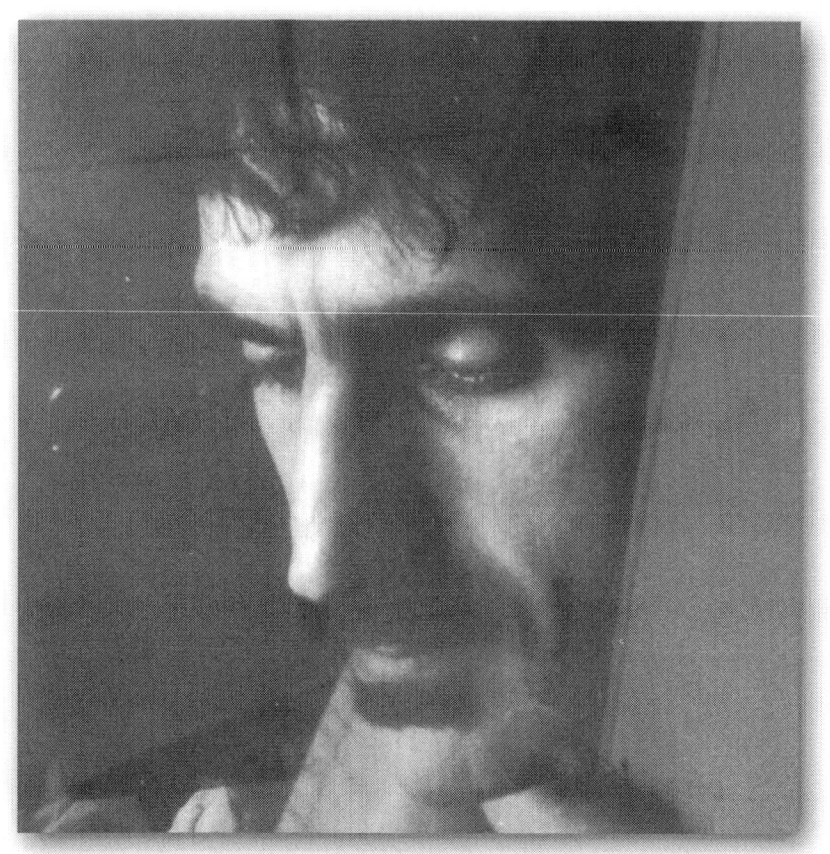

"One of my favorite photos of Frank."

New Jersey and California

On the evening of Sunday, December 5, 1993, I got a call from Gail.

I answered the phone, and she simply said, "Your brother is dead."

I didn't react immediately, and in the few moments of silence after her blunt statement, I collected my thoughts. Finally I said, "I'm sorry for your loss, Gail. When is the funeral?"

She replied in a flat monotone, "There isn't going to be a funeral. He's already been buried."

I was stunned. I asked when he died, and she said he had passed away on Saturday, December 4. I was trying to compute that. He died on Saturday and was buried the next day. I wanted to ask if Gail had called our mother, but I figured she had. I just hoped she had been a little less matter-of-fact about it with her.

Then she quickly said, "I have to go." And she hung up.

No other details, no further explanation, and no shared grief. At some point in our lives, we all experience the death of a loved one or a close friend. When that happens, kind and good people rally around each other and offer support and comfort. Gail's terse report was only the beginning of a series of events relating to Frank's death that have never been fully explained or resolved.

What's Next?

Gail's call left me with an overwhelming sense of loss. So many unanswered questions, so many disappointments, and so many missed opportunities. The litany of feelings was long and almost unbearable. But I knew that Frank's children were suffering more than I was because they were with him when he died. Like many of you, I have seen death up close and personal, and it leaves a mark on the soul.

Only after recently reconnecting with Moon and Dweezil am I aware of how much his death affected them. Their mother's passing was another blow, but not nearly as devastating as their father's.

For a few days after Gail's call, I was in a fog. At work, colleagues offered condolences. Friends from all around the country called or wrote notes to offer words of sympathy. After a week of dealing with the ambiguity of events relating to his death, I began to wonder about the circumstances. Yes, I knew he had died from prostate cancer, but what had been done to treat his disease? Where did he actually die? And of course, why was he buried so quickly?

When I called Mom, she was very upset but did her best to control her emotions. She said she was able to see Frank one last time when Gail had gone to visit her mother in Hawaii. She said it was a very emotional visit but one she would remember for the rest of her life.

After she had gotten her call from Gail, Mom said she couldn't eat and had trouble sleeping. The memory of seeing Frank in his final days haunted her. No parent should have to endure the emotional turmoil of losing a child, no matter how old. And no parent should have to go through what our mother did while Frank was alive and in treatment. She should have been able to have more contact with him, as should Candy, Carl, and I.

Practical Matters

After a while, Mom asked me to inquire about Frank's will. She and Carl were living in the duplex Frank bought our parents, and they believed it was theirs. Carl was living with Mom then and working at a fast-food restaurant. His life options were limited, but the home he and Mom shared for years was his secure base.

In June 1996, in an effort to find out what, if anything, Frank might have done to provide for Mom, Carl, Candy, and me, I contacted the lawyers who represented Frank's estate. I asked if there had been any provisions in Frank's will for us. In June, I received the following letter from one of the senior partners in response:

Dear Mr. Zappa:
    I have received and reviewed your letter of June 21, 1996, regarding the status of Frank Zappa's will. Please be advised that no probate was required for your brother's will due to the lack of any probate estate. I trust this answers your questions regarding the administration of your brother's will.

As you read this, some of you might think I was out of bounds by asking about Frank's will, that it makes me sound greedy in the wake of the grief and suffering his children and widow went through. But that was *three years earlier*. By 1996, our mother was in declining health, and I was worried about what would happen to Carl after she died.

After I received this letter, I wrote to the lawyer again and asked if it would be possible to get a written statement from the executor or administrator of Frank's estate clarifying whether any inheritance provisions were made in the trust fund (The Zappa Family Trust) for members of Frank's natural family or for any relatives outside of the Sloatman family.

On July 2, 1996, the lawyer wrote back, "Regarding the disposition of Frank Zappa's estate…please be advised that Frank's entire estate was left to his natural family, namely, his wife and four children. No provision was made for distributions to any other individuals."

And with that, Mom and Carl's living arrangement became clear. The legal message was that we should forget about any inheritance from Frank's estate. Mom was clearly disappointed, but she hoped that Gail would at least allow Carl to remain in the duplex until he got his life sorted out.

When Mom died in 2004, Gail moved quickly to sell the duplex, leaving Carl homeless. His secure base had vanished, his job at the fast-food restaurant was in jeopardy, and his life was in upheaval. Fortunately Candy lived nearby and was able to take Carl in until he could regroup and move in with a friend in San Diego, where he began to sort out his next moves.

How Did It Get This Fucked Up?

Frank was dead, Mom was dead, Carl was adrift, Candy was struggling on her own and trying to help Carl, and I was 2,900 miles away. The original Zappa family was crumbling, and I began to wonder how that had happened. The same questions that haunted me after Frank died came back in a rush: What had been done to treat his prostate cancer? Where did he actually die? What did the death certificate show? And of course, why was he buried so quickly?

It's no secret that Gail had issues with Frank's serial infidelities. Frank once told me about her fury over his sexual escapades, and now that he and Mom were gone and Carl was out of the way, Gail was in control. But there were still unanswered questions. I had to do something, find some answers, and get some closure.

Cold Cases

After Mom died, I thought of a way. Many large-city police departments have a cold case squad or department. They investigate older cases that have irregular or suspicious elements to see if a crime had been committed. Some of those cases are burglaries and others are murders, but any that are categorized as "cold" require special attention and greater detective work.

I wasn't sure if there was anything suspicious, in a criminal sense, about Frank's death, but I felt there were irregularities. I decided to contact the Los Angeles Police Department to see if there was any way to put my concerns to rest. I wrote to Chief William Bratton, asking if the LAPD could help answer my questions about Frank's death.

I didn't hear back for almost six months, but one day in late July, I got a call from Detective David Lambkin, head of the LAPD cold case squad. He said that Chief Bratton had given him my letter and asked him to follow up with me. He said he was going to assign my case to Detectives Rick Jackson and Tim Marcia and told me that Detective Jackson would be in touch soon. I was both thrilled and a bit nervous about this development because I didn't want to create a tempest in a shot glass, but apparently the LAPD thought it was worth looking into.

A few days later, Detective Jackson called. Rick Jackson is one of the LAPD's best-known investigators. He's known for his determination and accuracy, and he serves as the model for mega successful crime fiction author Michael Connelly, whose protagonist is Hieronymus Bosch, named after the fifteenth- and sixteenth-century painter whose view of hell on earth becomes a metaphor for the Los Angeles that Detective Jackson lived and worked in.

When Detective Jackson called, he asked me to tell him what I had written to Chief Bratton and why I had wanted to pursue the investigation. He said he read my letter to Bratton but wanted to hear it directly from me. This is what I told him.

This Is What Bothered Me

I began by pointing out that on Frank's death certificate, the place of death was listed as "residence," but the address given was 11917 Vose Street, a warehouse in the San Fernando Valley. In a conversation with Moon about this, she confirmed that he actually died at their house at 7885 Woodrow Wilson Drive. Why the discrepancy? Does it really matter if the location of a person's death is misstated on the death certificate?

Another nagging point had to do with the signature of the attending physician, whose name appeared next to the box on the death certificate that stated, "I certify that, to the best of my knowledge, Death occurred at the Hour, Date, and Place Stated from the Causes stated." Did that caveat absolve the attending physician from any misunderstanding about the actual time and place of death, even though certifying those details was that doctor's professional responsibility?

Apparently it doesn't really matter if such details are inaccurate. There was no autopsy shown or apparently required, and Frank was not embalmed, which was also not required. So how accurate was the statement that renal failure due to prostate cancer was the cause of death?

Another point, albeit a small one, was the description of the cause of death. It was given as renal failure due to "matastic" prostate cancer. The correct spelling is "metastatic." Does it really matter if the cause of death is misspelled?

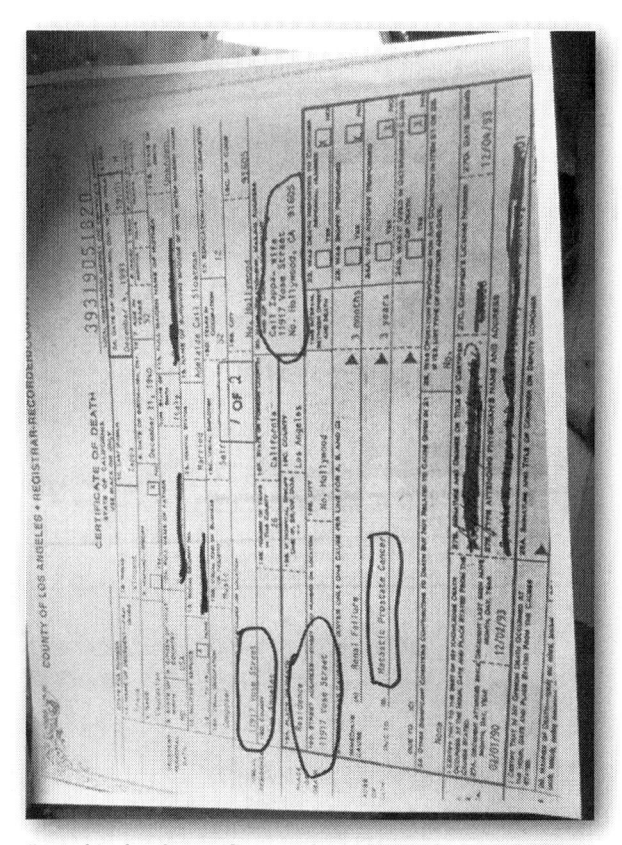

"Frank's death certificate. The circled information is the inconsistent data that led to the inquiry by the LAPD."

In a 2005 article in the journal *Histopathology* titled "Discrepancies between Clinical and Autopsy Diagnosis and the Value of Postmortem Histology: A Meta-Analysis and Review," researchers Roulson, Benbow, and Hasleton reported that "about one third of all death certificates are incorrect. Cause of death is one area where such errors occur."

Detective Jackson listened patiently to everything I told him and said he would get back to me. Several weeks later, he called, and we talked for about forty-five minutes. He said that the questions I raised did, in fact, suggest irregularities in the way Frank's death and burial were handled and reported. He said he spoke with several people during his investigation, and he concluded that, although further investigation was warranted, his department currently had over nine thousand open cold cases, and Frank's was simply not a priority.

I was disappointed but had no alternative but to let it go. I will never know exactly what treatments for prostate cancer Frank received, how they were conducted, or even when they were given. I will never know why he was buried without an autopsy to verify cause of death or why his burial happened so quickly.

Could Frank himself have established those conditions? This is something I will never know. And although it wasn't part of the investigation, I also wanted to know why there's no grave marker at Frank's burial plot. In fact, for almost three years after he died, my mother, Candy, Carl, and I had no idea where he was laid to rest. However, there has been speculation that Frank requested in his will that his grave remain unmarked. Is it possible that his self-esteem had sunk to such depths that he would disavow his own importance and deny so many relatives, fans, and friends the opportunity to honor him? This is also something I will never know. I have not seen the will, so I have no idea if this is true.

Candy happened to read an article that mentioned the cemetery where Frank was buried. She made time to go there (Westwood Memorial in Los Angeles, section D #100) and finally saw his unmarked grave.

While she was quietly standing over Frank's gravesite with a friend, someone from the cemetery came running up and told her she was not authorized to be there. My sister almost had to be restrained when she responded! It was unclear why instructions were given to deny Candy the right to pay her respects, but that only adds to the mystery surrounding his death.

Gail professed to love and care deeply about Frank, and she claimed it was her responsibility to guard him so ferociously with litigation, intimidation, and what some think was blind devotion. So it's hard to understand, let alone accept, the lack of public recognition she allowed after his passing without wondering what her real intent was.

This public statement from the Zappa Family Trust (ZFT) appeared in an article David Fricke wrote in *Rolling Stone* after Frank's death:

> The Zappa family has asked that anyone wishing to commemorate Zappa can make a donation in his name either to the Office for Intellectual Freedom of the American Library Association (50 East Huron, Chicago, IL 60611) or to the Cousteau Society, Greenpeace or any other favorite environmental cause. For those fans who are "financially restricted,"

just play his music if you are musicians, and otherwise play his music anyway. That will be enough for him.

When this was written in 1993, it may have confused people. Maybe this is why:

1. The inference is that the "Zappa family" is exclusively Frank's widow and his children. It fails to recognize his other original family members.
2. The "Zappa family" referenced in this notice appears to have given musicians permission to "play his music anyway."
3. Since Frank's death and the publication of this notice, gaining "permission to play his music" has now become a challenge because musicians who actually tried to play his music were faced with financial and legal obstacles.

Had the real intent been clearly spelled out initially, I think the notice should have read:

For those fans who are financially restricted, just find a way to buy the CDs and play his music (in the privacy of your own home) if you are musicians, and otherwise play his music anyway (but be sure to check the royalty rates before you do). That will be enough for him.

Well, maybe not for him, but clearly for some in the Zappa family.

15

Was Frank Zappa a Genius?

Eccentric, yes, genius, maybe.

—Frank Zappa, in response to Jamie Gangel's question during a *Today Show* interview, November 1993

Who Was He, and How Did He Get That Way?

In Frank's autobiography, *The Real Frank Zappa Book*, he said this about his ancestry:

> My ancestry is Sicilian, Greek, Arab, and French. My mother's mother was French and Sicilian, and her dad was Italian (from Naples). She was first generation. The Greek-Arab

side is from my dad. He was born in a Sicilian village called Partinico.

Why is it important to know this? Why, in fact, did Frank even mention it in his book? For one thing, our family's heritage is important to his children. I know firsthand that Moon and Dweezil are proud of their Italian roots. Their visit to Partinico in 2013 to see Salvo Cuccia's documentary about Frank's show in Palermo, Sicily, gave them the chance to meet their grandfather's relatives and experience the original Zappa family connections.

Frank's comment about his ancestry also made me curious about mine. So I took the Ancestry DNA test from Ancestry.com in 2016, and this what I found: 69 percent of my DNA comes from Italy and Greece, 4 percent from the Iberian Peninsula (Spain and Portugal), and 27 percent from West Asia (countries such as Syria, Lebanon, Iraq, Iran, Jordan, and Saudi Arabia).

Although Frank's assessment of his genetic heritage was based on his interpretation of historical more than empirical data, he was not far off. The question here is this: Did Frank's creativity and intelligence come from his ancestry? Would he have been any less (or more) brilliant if he were Swedish, Irish, or Polish? Conversely, can my genetic traits account for my own development?

I believe that the events that shaped Frank's view of the world were more important than his genes. Creativity may well have been in his DNA, but that quality was forged on the anvil of his real-world encounters. Going to jail on a trumped-up charge in Cucamonga was a factor. Being pushed into the orchestra pit in London was a factor. Confronting a group of senators in Washington about censorship was a factor. Being Italian-Greek-Arab-French may have sparked his intellectual development, but the hard, cold facts of his life encounters gave it form.

How Is "Genius" Defined?

People tend to throw the word genius around without really thinking about what it means. True geniuses are rare. In discussing James Gleick's book *Genius: The Life and Science of Richard Feynman*, writer Robby Berman suggests Gleick believes that geniuses have the ability to concentrate with intense interest and joy in mastering something and that getting good at something means spending a lot of time alone.

That succinctly described Frank Zappa. Frank also had traits like being outgoing and charming, the ability to devote time to solitary immersion in his work, and an intense interest in music that drove him away from a normal life. These were also the traits that his children experienced when Frank was working at home.

 Moon tells a story about wanting to spend time with her father because she had an idea for a song, and the only way she knew to get his attention was to slip a note under his studio door. She didn't dare disturb him by knocking or just walking in. She knew better.

 That night she went to bed after not hearing from him, but in the middle of the night, Frank woke her up and told her to come down to his studio. They began work on the song "Valley Girl" that night, and the rest is pop culture history. It was always on his terms and in his own time.

Early Music Interests That May Have Shaped Frank's Future

Back in the late 1950s and early 1960s, Frank identified with the black musicians who played the blues and who created some of the most enduring rock and roll ballads of all time. He and I spent countless hours together listening to records by the Penguins, the Dells, the Channels, and so many others, including Chuck Berry, Howlin' Wolf, Muddy Waters, Brownie McGhee, and Sonny Terry.

The simplicity and sincerity of those songs was comforting, energizing, and thoroughly entertaining for teenagers of that era. This was also when Frank developed a strong dislike of covers, like the McGuire Sisters' version of "Sincerely," which he saw as the white music industry's commercial exploitation of a black musician's original work. I think that became a factor in his determination to create his own musical identity, one that would define his musical genius, confound his critics, and challenge anyone who thought he or she could copy his unique and amazingly original compositions.

Developmental psychologists look at the circumstances, events, and outcomes over the life-span as a way to create theories of how people develop. Why and how, for example, can two people from the same family, with similar but not exactly the same genetic makeup, turn out so different? Why did Frank become an accomplished musician, and why did I go into publishing? How did Frank develop his amazing ability to think and verbalize opinions in any situation, while I take longer to process and respond? And what effect did Frank's commentary and social observations have on those who became lifelong fans of his music?

I doubt that there will ever be satisfactory answers to those questions. But one thing is certain: there is very little likelihood that someone with the same blend of Frank's unique artistic, intellectual, and emotion-generating talents and abilities will have the same profound impact on so many people. And from all that's been written about him, it seems I am not alone in that belief.

Things I Remember

As far back as I can remember, Frank and I were very close. As we got older, the bond was still there but not as intense. Life has a funny way of changing things we think will last forever. And so it was with Frankie and Bobby. Here are some thoughts on some of the good things.

His Incredible Talent

I was never jealous of Frank. I realized early on that he had gifts that I would never be able to duplicate or share. And I never wanted to. Frank demonstrated a clear sense of self-worth at an early age, and as I think back, there were many times when he tried to help me figure out my own self-worth.

His advice about working in New York for McGraw-Hill was a prime example. That advice, and my own growing confidence, helped me move out from behind his shadow. That was a major event in my life. He went his way, and I was able to find my own path.

His Intellect

From our days in Lancaster, where we were both outcasts, I was often awed by his ability to see through the nonsense that we experienced in high school. He stood his ground and taught me how to stand mine. He stood up to teachers and to our dad, and he showed me that I could do the same, which I did in later life, especially after I got out of the Marines.

He demonstrated by example how to deal with ignorant bigots, racists, and conservatives whose only motivation was to demean anyone who didn't agree with their views. He could outthink, outspeak, and out-reason anyone who challenged him. And in the process, he could support his positions with statistics, data, and facts. He set the bar high for all of us who were subject to that kind of harassment, and so many of his fans learned from him, as I did.

His Sense of Humor

Anyone who has seen him in concert knows that humor had a very important place in his music. I have seen many concerts, and in every one of them, Frank gave the distinct impression that he was having one hell of a good time interacting with his audiences. There were times when he laughed uncontrollably when Jimmy Carl Black or Jim "Motorhead" Sherwood did something so outrageous onstage that he was blown away by their antics.

I remember one time in Lancaster when we were on our way to see Don Cerveris, our high-school English teacher. This is what Frank said in his autobiography:

My English teacher at A.V. was Don Cerveris. He was also a good friend. Don got tired of being a teacher and quit—he wanted to be a screenwriter. In 1959, he wrote the screenplay for a super-cheap cowboy movie called *Run Home Slow* and helped me get my first film-scoring job on it.

On our way to Don's house that night, we walked by a clothing store on the main drag in Lancaster. Frank said he wanted to go in and look around. So we walked around looking at clothes, which I didn't find unusual, but what I didn't know was that he was looking for something in particular.

We ended up in the women's department and came upon the section with bras. Instead of full-length mannequins, the store used plastic chests to exhibit them. Frank found one that was bra-less and slipped it under his coat. He closed his coat, and we left the store. Nobody noticed or seemed to care that we had just stolen some plastic tits.

Frank told me that when we got to Don's house, I should pretend that some bullies had been chasing us and then let him do the rest. When we got there, Frank rang the doorbell, and when Don opened the door, we bolted in, pretending to be out of breath. Don asked what was wrong, and Frank said we had just been chased as he plopped down on the sofa.

Don went to the door and looked out to see who was following us, but of course, no one was there. When Don turned around, Frank had unbuttoned his coat, and the plastic tits were sticking out under his shirt.

Don looked at them for a minute and then started to laugh hysterically, as did Frank and I. I guess you had to be there. Frank loved to laugh, though, and when he did, you couldn't help but laugh with him.

Now the Downside: Who's in Charge?

In most successful marriages, there's a sense of shared responsibility. The husband is often the breadwinner, and the wife is often the homemaker. Yes, I know those role models aren't the norm today, but for the sake of argument, hear me out.

What many of us have difficulty understanding is why that particular model didn't work for Frank. Maybe it was because he was on the road sometimes as much as seven months a year. Perhaps it was because he was so intensely focused on his music that he didn't have time to be husband, father, and neighborhood backyard BBQ guy. Or maybe it was because, over time, he began to see that his marriage wasn't working.

But whatever it was that affected his relationship with his wife and kids, prior to his cancer, he seemed to relinquish his authority as the head of his own household. My perception of that stems from his growing isolation from his parents and siblings; the upheaval in his business world in the form of lawsuits, demoralized and displaced band members, and support staff; and his increasing involvement in social and political issues.

Maybe he was looking for new challenges. The Parents Music Resource Center Senate hearings and his contact with Vaclav Havel in Prague were clearly a departure from his music. The question is why. What motivated him to reinvent himself? Was he just disaffected with the music business, or was he actually pursuing an interest in politics? Or was he trying to find new ways to avoid becoming a stay-at-home husband and dad?

Obviously he didn't give up on the things he did best. He still wrote music, he was still involved with digital technology and sound reproduction, and he still maintained an interest in visual media. But he seemed restless, even anxious about the future. We'll never know what motivated him at that point in his life, but whatever it was, he was becoming a different person.

His transformation from rock icon into social and political gadfly posed more questions than will ever be answered. And while many of his fans probably see that transformation as the normal course of events in his amazing career, I, and many others wonder about the reasons behind it. Any clues to that are long gone, though, like so many things that we'll never know about Frank's last years and final days.

16

Frank Zappa: Tributes and Honors

*The people most offended by my
lyrics seem to be rock critics.*

—Frank Zappa, *The Real Frank Zappa Book*

IN THE RESORT community of Bad Doberan, eastern Germany, the Zappanale music festival has been held each year since 1990. Various bands from all over the world play music by Frank Zappa. Many of the musicians who perform at this festival have previously played with Frank's band.

The festival's organizers are from what was once East Germany and grew up during a time when Frank's music was considered unacceptable, even subversive, in Eastern European communist countries. In fact, the Stasi, the official state security police in East Germany, which has been described as one of the most effective and repressive intelligence agencies ever created, actively watched Wolfhard Kutz because he was a Zappa fan. Wolfhard was one of the founders of the Zappanale, and he remains active in the festival today.

When the Berlin Wall fell in 1989, Kutz was finally able to listen freely to Frank's music. In 1992, after all of the Stasi files on subversive activity were declassified by the German government, Kutz found that his file stated that he "knows how to influence the youth with Zappa." In 1993, the year Frank died, Kutz and his friend Thomas Dippel formed the Arf Society, an officially registered German entity that now coordinates the Zappanale.

Another key member of the Zappanale organization is Jim Cohen. He has been the Zappanale's volunteer emcee since 1999, when he gave his first presentation there. Jim has a bachelor's and master's in linguistics and knows at least five languages. He lives in Munich and works as a technical translator and teacher. I have done two Skype interviews with Jim, most recently in 2015, when he did his presentation on Frank in the theater in Bad Doberan.

In 2002, the organizers helped raise money to have Czech sculptor Vaclav Cesak make a bronze bust of Frank, which is now prominently placed at the entrance to Bad Doberan. That year, Bill Harris and I were invited to the festival to participate in its unveiling. That was when Bill told the audience to rub Frank's nose for good luck. That was also the first year my sister, Candy, performed at the Zappanale with Ed Palermo's Big Band, a group of enormously talented musicians who have established a wide following and a well-earned reputation for performing Frank's most complex orchestral pieces.

My son, Stanley Jason Zappa, played saxophone at the 2008 Zappanale along with drummer Nick Skrowaczewski, son of the late conductor of the Minnesota Orchestra, Stanislaw Skrowaczewski. Candy's second time at the festival was in 2016 with her husband, Nolan Porter, when they performed with former Mothers band member Denny Walley and the Muffin Men.

The Zappanale organizers, Thomas Dippel and Wolfhard Kutz, have established a solid relationship with the musical members of the Zappa family. In fact, in 2017, Dweezil is scheduled to perform at the festival to celebrate this incredible tribute to his father.

The Fly in the Ointment

In November 2007, the Zappa Family Trust sued the festival for use of the Zappa name and image without permission. In August 2008, court hearings were held in Düsseldorf with the goal of reaching an out-of-court settlement.

The Zappa Family Trust wanted to be paid for any merchandise sold at the festival that used the Zappa logo (Frank's mustache and bull string) and also wanted €150,000 in damages plus another €250,000 for any future sales of merchandise using the Zappa logo.

After deliberating, the court found that the Zappa Family Trust, which at the time was headed by Gail Zappa, was unable to prove that it actively uses its trademark in Germany, a requirement to win such lawsuits. In addition, the court ruled that the differences between the official Zappa logo and the one used by the Zappanale were great enough to preclude confusion of the two.

When the verdict was handed down, Thomas Dippel, then head the Arf Society, told the German newspapers that he was "very satisfied" and was looking forward to the twentieth anniversary of the festival to be held that summer. In 2008, almost ten thousand fans attended. I suspect, with Dweezil's participation in 2017, the crowd will be enormous.

A Scholarly Examination of Frank's Life

Musicians and current fans make up only one component of Frank's growing legion of followers. There are courses that explore his life, commentary, and music at high schools and colleges around the country. The professors who teach the college courses are bringing in a new generation of converts to the Frank Zappa fan base. One of the most prominent and longest running of these courses is "The Music of Frank Zappa," taught by Dr. Joseph Klein, distinguished teaching professor and department chairman since 1999 at the University of North Texas in Denton, Texas.

In recent years, Dr. Klein's course has focused on the bigger picture of American history, culture, and society in the second half of the twentieth century. He believes that Frank directly addressed so many important social and political issues through his music and interviews that students come away from class knowing a lot more about the historical period in which Frank lived. Another course is called "Frank Zappa and Media Bias," taught by Professor Jon Nelson at the State University of New York in Buffalo. Professor Nelson is a Julliard-trained trumpet player and has been teaching at SUNY Buffalo since 1998. In his course, he examines Frank's music, the social context in which it was written, and how it relates to today's political climate.

Frank has also received other types of recognition. In 1988, he won a Grammy for *Jazz from Hell*. In 1995, he was inducted posthumously into the Rock and Roll Hall of Fame. Also in 1995, a cast of Frank created by a Lithuanian sculptor Konstantinas Bogdanas was placed in the center of the capital of Lithuania. Biologist Ed Murdy named a genus of gobiid fishes of New Guinea *Zappa*. Not to be outdone, biologist Ferdinando Boero named a jellyfish after Frank. Frank's also had fossils, spiders, bacteria, asteroids, and video game characters named after him. There's even a Frank Zappa Appreciation Day held every year in Baltimore, Maryland.

"This is the bronze bust of Frank created by sculptor Vaclav Cesak. It sits at the entrance to the village of Bad Doberon in eastern Germany. The shiny nose is the result of Bill Harris's suggestion to rub it for good luck."

Fifteen Minutes of Fame

My trip to Bad Doberan for the 2002 Zappanale and my participation in the unveiling of the bronze bust are still strong, pleasant memories for me. I had not yet published my first book, and I felt like I didn't really belong there. I mean, I didn't think I had any real purpose for attending at the promoter's expense, other than the fact that Frank and I were brothers. At least Candy performed with Ed Palermo. All I did was make a speech, give a few interviews, and meet with fans. They didn't seem to mind my lack of talent, though, and for that I'm grateful.

"In 2002 I attended the thirteenth annual Zappanale music festival. Here I am with Pierrejean Gaucher and Christoph Godin, two French guitarists who performed that year."

But 2002 was a bittersweet year. The 9/11 attack was a year earlier, America was on edge about terrorism, President Bush was getting ready to go to war, and people all over the world were shaken to their core when they realized that, as Frank once taunted, "it can't happen here," but it surely did. For me, the Zappanale gave respite from the growing fears about the future and allowed me to relive moments with Frank that had gotten dusty from lack of use.

"At the 2002 Zappanale with Bill Harris (partially hidden). Courtesy of Angel Tejeda."

By the end of the festival, my fond memories and enthusiasm about my life with Frank had been reinvigorated. That was when I went back to writing, with the goal of trying to describe, through my lens, just how amazing my brother was. And looking back, I think Frank would have enjoyed knowing he had that kind of influence on so many people, even though it was something he did not believe was essential to a productive and successful career. I also think he would be pleased to know that he is not only remembered but still honored in so many ways.

17

Reconnecting with Moon and Dweezil

The more boring a child is, the more the parents, when showing off the child, receive adulation for being good parents—because they have a tame child-creature in their house.

—FRANK ZAPPA

New York City

THE LAST TIME I saw Moon and Dweezil was in 1974 at an Easter egg hunt at Frank's house on Woodrow Wilson Drive. Gail had invited several families with little children. There was a guy running around in a white bunny costume, and his job was to hide eggs and try not to scare the kids. There were snacks, plenty of candy, wine, and soda.

I remember Frank coming out to the yard about thirty minutes into the party, but he didn't stay long. He said a few words to the guests and then something to Gail, and then he came to me and said he was working on something and had to get back to his studio. So much for parental involvement!

Our son, Jason, and Dweezil were running around like army ants. Moon was busy playing with the little girls in the group. Ahmet was wandering around, looking for Easter eggs. And most of the parents were standing around getting bored. It was a typically perfect Los Angeles afternoon, with bright sun, moderate temperatures, and an abundance of self-important Hollywood Hills people. Most were there as much to be seen as to prove to the others what good moms and dads they were for giving up an afternoon for their little ones. After about two hours of watching the kids grow tired and cranky, not unlike their parents, Marcia, Jason, and I went home.

Not long after that party, the key events that changed my life began to take shape. My father passed away in April 1973. Mom was living with Carl and Candy in their duplex, and I was getting signals from the New York office about a possible promotion to an editorial assignment. Frank was touring all over the world, and Los Angeles was losing its appeal as the Promised Land for anyone who wasn't in show business, especially me. I was anxious to move on.

The flurry of activity in Frank's world and the job realignment in mine made it difficult for us to keep in regular contact. And while he was on the road, Gail was busy with her own life, so contact with her and their children was, at best, infrequent. As Frank became more famous, we were not included in any of their other social gatherings. That meant that our children were losing touch with each other too.

And in July 1975, I was offered the physics editor's job. In August, we packed up and moved to New Jersey so I could start work in the New York office of McGraw-Hill. As of this writing, it's been twenty-three years since my brother died. In that time, a series of events have altered the lives of Frank's own family and those of his four children. Some of those events and the people who made them happen brought out the worst in those affected, and at times they brought out the best. Here are my thoughts.

Gail (Sloatman) Zappa

I met Gail in New York in 1967 when I worked for Frank at the Garrick Theater. She was pregnant with their daughter Moon, and when Frank introduced us, I got the immediate impression that she did not like me. I didn't understand why at the time, but over the years, her attitude never changed. In fact it got worse. This is how I think it started.

One night I stopped by their apartment on Thompson Street after the show, and her father was also there. He and Frank were talking about the Vietnam War, and they had different opinions about it. Frank thought it was a waste of time, money, and lives. Gail's father thought it was justified because of the domino theory. I jumped in and said it was bullshit and was going to get a lot worse before it got any better.

Her father and I disagreed, and as one thing led to another, we started yelling. Okay, so I might have been a little drunk, but so was he. Anyway, I realized that from that point on, my relationship with Gail had gone off the rails, and fixing it was not an option. But in my defense, as difficult as she was to deal with, she was the mother of Frank's children, and I did my best to be civil around her. She did not return the courtesy.

When I think about Frank, the biggest regret I have is not having seen him the week I was in Los Angeles. I was there specifically to spend time with my brother. But for whatever reason, Gail kept putting me off until it was too late, and I had to get back to New Jersey. I will also never understand why Frank didn't ask for me, or if he did, what he was told. Maybe by then she was more concerned with Frank's rapidly declining health than allowing us one last visit. Or maybe she was afraid I'd ask Frank questions about his estate. In fact, had we gotten together, I would have asked him about the status of the duplex he bought for our parents, the one Mom and Carl lived in, the same duplex Gail sold only days after our mother's death in 2004, which left Carl adrift without a home.

For many years, I struggled to understand Gail's attitude toward Candy, Carl, Mom, and me, and I kept coming back to one theme. I think she wanted to make Frank comfortable in his final days, but she was equally determined to get retribution for his on-the-road relationships. We were obstacles that had to be dispatched in order for her to resolve her feelings about him. I also think she believed she had the right and the business sense to use Frank's wealth and extensive music library as she saw fit. At the end of her life, neither appears to have been the case.

FRANKIE & BOBBY: THE REST OF OUR STORY

In June 2016, I had the great pleasure of reconnecting with my niece Moon after four decades. She was in New York to help promote the documentary *Eat That Question*. The night she came for dinner, we talked for hours about her life with Frank, Gail, Dweezil, Ahmet, and Diva. She asked me about my son, Jason, and she wanted to know about Carl and Candy. We covered a lot of territory that evening, some of it disturbing.

She asked if some of the things her mother had told her were true. Specifically, why didn't I want to have contact with her and the other kids? She said Gail told them I was living the "high life" in New York, working for a big publishing company, and couldn't be bothered with them. And she asked why I didn't want to see Frank before he died. And did Gail really pay for all of my son's medical expenses when he had cancer?

When she asked those questions, I was shocked. All I could say was that her mother had not told her the truth, and of course I wanted to have a relationship with them. As for living the "high life" in New York publishing, Gail pulled that one out of thin air. I worked in educational publishing selling textbooks. Not a lot of glamour in that. And the biggest lie was that she paid for Jason's medical bills. She did nothing of the sort. Jason's own health insurance and our out-of-pocket contributions did that.

After we cleared the air about those falsehoods, Moon told me about the difficulties she and Dweezil were having with Ahmet and the Zappa Family Trust. Some of it we'd heard the month before when Dweezil and his wife, Megan, came to lunch. Here's how that went.

Dweezil Zappa

Like his sister, Dweezil asked why I didn't want to have contact with him and Moon. I told him the same thing I told Moon, and I added that I would also like to connect with Ahmet and Diva. But after learning about how Ahmet was handling the Zappa Family Trust and the problems that have arisen for Moon and Dweezil, that reunion is unlikely.

"With Dweezil in New York."

Dweezil explained how Gail used Frank's money to pay legal fees for lawsuits that she unsuccessfully waged. He said she reneged on the bequest in Frank's will to leave his guitars to Dweezil and instead put them up for auction to help raise money to pay her own debts. He also said that before Frank died, he wrote a letter to each of his children. Dweezil never got his because Gail refused to give it to him.

There were other stories about Gail's actions through the trust that have created significant issues for Dweezil and Moon. The litany was disturbing, hard to fathom, and seemingly impossible to resolve. But what I do know from my reunion with my niece and nephew is this:

1. Moon is a beautiful, intelligent, and talented young woman, a successful published author, stand-up comic, and actor. She misses her father, has difficulty with how her mother treated her and Dweezil, and is happy to be back in touch with me. She is charming, funny, and loving. She is actively writing, performing, and doing promotion work in Hollywood and abroad. And she is the mother of a beautiful daughter whose birthday is December 21, the same day as Frank's.

"Another photo of Moon and me."

2. Dweezil is the legitimate (and only) heir to Frank's musical legacy. He has become a guitar virtuoso in his own right. He has Frank's gift for thinking and speaking clearly. He is amazingly intelligent, verbally agile, and genuinely kind. I have met many people who have been to his concerts.

Those who have met him all say he is a gentleman, grateful for his fan base, and down to earth, even though he is now one of the most important figures on the rock music scene. He too has successfully emerged from a dysfunctional home life, and with his wife, Megan, he is creating his own secure base as a husband, father of two daughters, and stepfather to Megan's daughter.

On Sunday, October 30, 2016, I went to my first Dweezil concert. It was at the Beacon Theater in Manhattan, and it was amazing. When I got to the theater, Megan and Dweezil met me in the lobby. There were hugs all around, and then we went upstairs to their private backstage room, where we had a chance to talk and have a bite to eat.

"Megan and Dweezil Zappa at our apartment in New York"

Dweezil filled me in on the ZFT's latest efforts, confirming for me at least that jealousy and greed are its driving force. He said the trust has petitioned to have the name "Zappa" trademarked, citing every possible product, media format, entertainment effort, and anything else the trust's lawyers could list to fall under its magic spell. As of this writing, Dweezil and Moon are contesting the Zappa Family Trust's trademark petition.

"The Beacon Theater, October 30, 2016."

FRANKIE & BOBBY: THE REST OF OUR STORY

When it came time for the show, Megan and I went down to our seats, where we met with my wife's daughter, Anna Finlay. The theater was packed, and the crowd was in a good mood. Many were wearing Halloween costumes, much as it was when Frank did his Halloween show in New York City back in the day.

When the band came onstage, the crowd began to cheer, but when Dweezil came out, they went wild.

I saw Frank and the Mothers perform many times, and the audience reaction was very similar. Frank represented so much to so many of his fans, and Dweezil has assumed the same mantle. He is Frank personified in so many ways, and the show that night only confirmed it for me. At times during the show, I closed my eyes and saw Frank playing. That's how good Dweezil is.

Under his direction, his band has duplicated the precision and range that some of the best of Frank's groups achieved. It's no small feat, as many of you who have seen Frank and Dweezil perform already know.

Anyone who knows what traveling musicians go through understands that it's a hard life. Rarely do things go smoothly. Grace under pressure is difficult. Yet Dweezil has mastered that. I have seen him be gracious, kind, friendly, funny, patient, and courteous with fans. Frank was the same way, most of the time. Dweezil is that way all of the time. And I am very proud to be his uncle.

So many of Frank's devoted fans have reached out to me, expressing their feelings about how Frank helped them in difficult periods of their own lives through his music and social commentary. On a very personal level, I understand how they feel. My brother was my best friend and my hero. His honesty, bravery, and brilliance helped me too, simply by his being my big brother. All the other things he was and did were just icing on the cake.

And to this day Moon, Dweezil, along with me so many others, we still miss him every day.

"*October 30, 2016 backstage at the Beacon Theater before Dweezil's show.*"

18

Bob Zappa Today

My younger brother Bobby picked up a cowboy-style, arch-top, F-hole guitar at an auction for $1.50 and started playing it.

—FRANK ZAPPA, THE REAL FRANK ZAPPA BOOK

"Frankie and Bobby in Edgewood, Maryland circa 1946."

IN AUGUST 2015, I self-published my memoir, *Frankie & Bobby: Growing Up Zappa*, and since then, I've been amazed at the reactions. Without trying to sound too self-absorbed, I'd like to share some other things about my life. Feel free to ignore this chapter, though. I won't be offended.

Up and Out

In the publishing business, as in many other businesses in America, the meter starts running the minute you start work. Productivity is king, and survivors learn quickly how to play the game. Looking back, I had a good run in the world of words. I worked for McGraw-Hill until things went south and I found myself on the street. Fortunately my contacts in the business helped me get reemployed in a series of jobs with other publishers like Macmillan, Prentice-Hill, Simon & Schuster, Primedia, and finally a small family-run (now defunct) publisher called Oceana, which was my last job in the industry.

Start to finish, I spent thirty-plus years in book publishing—in sales, editorial, marketing, and general management. I held positions in the United States and abroad. I learned a lot about old-school book publishing, but as technology changed the rules, those changes overtook me, and I failed to keep pace. But by then, I was tired of the bullshit, the posturing, and the competitive grind.

So one morning in May 2001, after a particularly thorny argument with my boss, I left my last job in publishing. Having been through the drill a few times before, this one was easy and actually a relief. I even went to a diner on my way home and had lunch. I felt good about leaving the stress, competition, and confusion behind, but I now faced a new challenge: avoiding financial, marital, and emotional ruin.

What Next?

One thing I learned about working in business in America, at least for me, is that you get so immersed in making a living that life has a way of passing you by. Okay, that sounds corny, but for me, it was true: up early, long hours commuting, long hours at a desk, unrewarding activity on the job, and sparse family time. It all really sucked by the end, but being out of work at fifty-nine was no way to end a career. I had to regroup, adapt, and improvise.

In June 2001, I started exploring alternative job opportunities. Being a Walmart greeter looked doable. I knew being a Home Depot sales clerk would have been a little tougher, unless they had a book section. Crossing guard, grocery bagger, and janitor were also looking like attractive options, but I guess I wanted something more, something I could really sink my teeth into. Then it hit me.

Are You "Fellows" Material?

I found a program on the New York City Department of Education website (DOE) that looked really interesting. Without it, I would have never been able to achieve the most life-altering career change I could have ever made. I decided to try to become a New York City Teaching Fellow. Here's a little background on the Teaching Fellows program from their website:

> In the spring of 2000, the NYC Teaching Fellows program was launched to address…a chronic shortage of qualified teachers, with nearly 11,000 uncertified teachers working in the district, disproportionately teaching in the city's highest-need schools…The Fellowship recruits and selects accomplished professionals and recent graduates with the academic expertise to teach critical shortage subjects.

FRANKIE & BOBBY: THE REST OF OUR STORY

Actually I think the main purpose of the program was to hire out-of-work business types like me who needed a job with a steady income, retirement, and health benefits. We were supposed to replace older, much higher paid, and, in some cases, fully burned-out teachers who used movies as their primary instructional media while they caught up on their midday naps or the *Daily News* crossword puzzles.

I decided to apply to the program. I didn't exactly meet all their criteria, but what probably impressed them was my time in the Marine Corps. One day I got a letter telling me that I had been chosen to go to the next level in the application process. I seem to recall that the number of applicants in 2002 was somewhere around sixteen thousand. Of that number, approximately twenty-four hundred were selected, and by the time all steps had been completed in the screening process, only sixteen hundred or so actually made it into the school system. I was in that group.

The next step was to attend a job fair where principals or their representatives from what were called hard-to-staff schools gathered to interview new Teaching Fellows. While not exactly a meat market, the screening was a little bit like a livestock auction: check teeth, squeeze biceps, and look for signs of weakness in character or visible scaredy-catness.

Having never been to a poor neighborhood in New York City, let alone a hard-to-staff school, I was eager to demonstrate my willingness to face hostile fire, having had some experience in that area. After only three interviews, I was offered a job. My gender, race, and military background probably all played favorably in the decision.

The school I would be teaching at was in the Sound View section of the Bronx. It was a middle school that served first and second and then sixth through eighth grades. The logic behind this lineup was unclear to me, but it didn't really matter. I mean, I didn't really care what the grades were because I had absolutely no idea of what was ahead.

What I later learned, though, was that teachers in the lowest grades often ended their day smelling of pee and poop, while those of us in the higher grades might end up with bruises and smelling of preteen hormonal effluvia. Think of actually seeing hormones whipping around in the classroom, followed by explosive violence, bizarre, and sexually charged behavior. You had to be there to fully understand.

Once the selection process was completed and I was hired as a full-time New York City Teaching Fellow, I had to register for graduate classes at Lehman College of the City University of New York, where I would earn my master's degree in education.

Meanwhile, I was actually supposed to start "teaching" at my new school. That began in June 2002. Summer school was under way, and I was assigned to work with a teacher who taught a remedial class in US history to seventh graders who had failed that class during the school year. I realized after several weeks on the job that most of my colleagues were dedicated teachers who genuinely liked their students. The younger teachers had a level of optimism that was surprisingly refreshing. Those who had been at the school much longer were much less motivated, and this attitude was not lost on the kids.

Fast-Forward

After two years in the middle school, I transferred to a high school in another part of the Bronx. That was a major transition. High-school kids were easier to teach, but their level of sophistication about how to weasel out of their wrongdoing was stunning. I learned what it meant for kids to be street-smart and street-tough at that school. After eleven and a half years in the New York City school system, I think I got a little more street-smart myself but not nearly as tough as my students.

There were times when I'd felt safer in the Marine Corps than I did at my school. I taught at the old Morris High School, a five-story Gothic building. General Colin Powell had graduated from Morris, but by the time I got there, it was a far different place.

Mine was one of five separate small public schools in the building, each with its own principal, assistant principal, teaching staff, paraprofessionals, and New York City school cops. We had four cops on our floor off and on throughout the day. They were there to assist teachers when students got out of control, which was daily, sometimes hourly.

The small-school model was supposed to allow for smaller classes and more tutorial contact between teacher and student, and this was supposed to lead to higher graduation rates and college admissions. But in fact, as soon as the city set up a small school, the DOE would send more students than the original plan called for, mirroring the classroom overcrowding that the larger schools experienced.

But it wasn't all psychodrama. In the summer of 2012, I was selected to participate in the Congressional Fellows program in Washington, DC. The program brings in US history teachers from around the country to learn firsthand the basics of how laws are proposed and passed. We also met some of the congressional representatives and senators who do the daily business of government. I had the distinct honor of meeting Congressman John Lewis, the civil rights legend. He was elected to Congress in the 5th District in Georgia in 1986 and for the past 30 years has been recognized for his distinguished service in office. His background, achievements, and awards are among the most impressive of any elected official in the federal government. He is a kind, generous, and thoughtful man whose contributions to our democracy have set the bar high for every other elected official, even the president.

FRANKIE & BOBBY: THE REST OF OUR STORY

"I met Congressman and civil rights legend John Lewis during my participation in the Congressional Fellows program in 2012 in Washington, DC."

Good teachers know if they have connected with students. They recognize signs of maturity, intellectual growth, and personal responsibility. I considered myself an average teacher, but after almost twelve years of working with hundreds of students in one of the toughest neighborhoods in the Bronx, I think I can say that I may have helped a few. That's not false modesty, though. I have not had contact with many of my former students since I retired, so I can't give many specific examples. I just have hope that I made a difference.

How Things Change

In 2013, my wife of forty-eight years, Marcia, passed away from pancreatic cancer. It was, as anyone who has lost a spouse knows, a major stress factor. But I was very fortunate to reconnect with someone I'd known many years before who came back into my life.

I met Diane Papalia in 1985 when I worked for McGraw-Hill. I was a marketing manager then, and she was one of the college division's best-selling textbook authors in psychology, human, and child development. I marketed her books.

At that time, she was also a professor at the University of Wisconsin–Madison, but when we reconnected in late 2013, she was by then divorced and living alone in New York City. That was also when I decided to retire from teaching. We both realized that our lives would be a lot fuller together, so in September 2015, we were married. We had our wedding and reception at the Plaza Athénée hotel in New York City and were delighted to have seventy guests help us celebrate.

"Anna Finlay, Diane's daughter and maid of honor at our wedding in 2015. Courtesy of Maggie Yuracheck."

"My wife, Diane, and me in the Plaza Athénée lobby after our wedding." Photo courtesy of Maggie Yuracheck.

It was a great event for us, and we truly enjoyed sharing the evening with our friends. Diane and I now live in a prewar condo on the Upper West Side of Manhattan. I consider myself extremely fortunate to have been able to reinvent my life with Diane after so many twists and turns over the years. And as I write this, I can't help but think that Frank would have been happy for me, maybe even proud that I may have actually "made it" in New York. And I couldn't have done that without his snarky advice and brotherly love.

A Few Last Words

Frank, wherever you are, here are a few things I want you to know:

1. I miss you and hope you are in a much better place.
2. I hope you have room service there.
3. I'm sorry I hit you with that croquet mallet at Aunt Mary's.
4. I'm sorry I wasn't with you in London.
5. I hope we can be together again one day.

Finally, if you were alive today, I know you could have been elected president.

About the Authors

BOB ZAPPA is Frank Zappa's younger brother by three years. In 1961, after graduating from high school in Claremont, California, he joined the United States Marine Corps. His first deployment was with the Second Battalion, First Marine Regiment during the Cuban Missile Crisis. In 1965, as part of the Third Battalion, Seventh Marine Regiment, he participated in the first action taken in South Vietnam after the Gulf of Tonkin incident.

After serving in the Marines, Bob earned a bachelor's degree in history from California State Polytechnic University in Pomona, California, a research diploma in social psychology from the University of Stockholm, Sweden, and a master's degree in education from the City University of New York at Lehman College in the Bronx. In 2002, he joined the New York City Teaching Fellows program, teaching at a high school in the South Bronx. He taught US history and economics at the School for Excellence at the Morris High School campus, General Colin Powell's alma mater.

He is now retired and living in Manhattan with his wife, Diane Papalia.

Bob's coauthor, **Diane E. Papalia**, graduated from Vassar College and later earned her PhD in life-span developmental psychology from West Virginia University. For many years, she was a professor of child and family studies at the University of Wisconsin–Madison, where she taught undergraduate and graduate courses in human development. She also coauthored several college textbooks on child and human development and introduction to psychology that are used around the world and have been translated into several languages.

Made in the USA
San Bernardino, CA
26 October 2017

Made in the USA
San Bernardino, CA
26 October 2017